LINCOLN

AS THE SOUTH SHOULD KNOW HIM

O. W. Blacknall

Foreword by Walter D. Kennedy and James R. Kennedy
Edited by Frank B. Powell, III

Can the man who suffered his lieutenant, Sherman, to ruthlessly devastate twice as much Southern territory as all Belgium combined be the Southern ideal?

Can the man whose life work was to tear from the Declaration of Independence its immortal part, its very soul, "That governments derive their just powers from the consent of the governed," be the American ideal, if the truth is looked full in the face?

FOURTH EDITION

REPRINTED BY
The Scuppernong Press
Wake Forest, NC
www.scuppernongpress.com

Lincoln as the South Should Know Him
By O. W. Blacknall
Foreword by Walter D. Kennedy and James R. Kennedy
Edited by Frank B. Powell, III

©2011 The Scuppernong Press

First Printing

The Scuppernong Press
PO Box 1724
Wake Forest, NC 27588
www.scuppernongpress.com

Cover and book design by Frank B. Powell, III

All rights reserved.
Printed in the United States of America.

No part of this book maybe reproduced or transmitted in any form or by any means, electronic or mechanical, including photocopying, recording, or by any information and storage and retrieval system, without written permission from the editor and/or publisher.

International Standard Book Number
                    ISBN 978-0-9845529-6-2

Library of Congress Control Number: 2011934618

Contents

Foreword .... *iii*

Introduction .... *vii*

Lincoln as the South Should Know Him 1

Biography of O. W. Blacknall 37

Burning of Columbia, SC — February 17, 1865

Foreword

Few men in America can elicit such patriotic emotion as that of the sixteenth president of the United States, Abraham Lincoln. Yet to the South of 1860 and unreconstructed Southerners, Lincoln is an enigma of American history. O. W. Blacknall is emblematic of the unreconstructed Southerner as his 1915 work on Lincoln, *Lincoln as the South Should Know Him,* demonstrates.

In 1991 the Kennedy Twins of Louisiana wrote *The South Was Right!* From that year to this year, more than 125,000 copies of that book have been sold. Of all the issues which are discussed in that now well-read book, the one issue that seems to cause more consternation has been the issue of who is the real Lincoln. Is Lincoln the man of racial justice and equality or is he the man who believed in White supremacy and Negro inferiority? Is Lincoln the man who freed the slaves or the man who offered security for the slave property of slave-holders if said slave-holders would support his war? Is Lincoln the defender of the Union or the man who destroyed the Union as established by our founding fathers? Is Lincoln the advocate of limited, i.e., Constitutional, government or the man who made big government not only possible but inevitable in these United States? These answers and many others were answered by O. W. Blacknall in 1915 and reasserted by the Kennedy Twins in 1991. Still too many Americans kneel before the icon of Lincoln and worship the man who the South feared and only 39 percent of Americans voted for in 1860. When dealing with the enigma of Lincoln one often finds the most ironic mixture of Lincoln defenders. For example, the co-founders of modern-day communism, Karl Marx and Fredrick Engels both supported Lincoln's war against the South. Marx wrote articles and led demonstrations against the Confederate States of America in Europe, while incorrectly proclaiming the South was seeking to defend and promote slavery. Thus today, we will hear conservative talking heads on television and radio proclaiming how great it was that Lincoln prevented the states of the South from "keeping slavery alive in America." Fredrick Engels praised the idea of destroying small republics (states) and combining said states into one large "indivisible" republic because this would promote the communist revolution. These same conservative talking heads will joyously proclaim how great it was that Lincoln's War produced "one nation indivisible." How ironic, America's conservative talking heads sound more like Marxist sycophants than defenders of the Constitution, limited government and individual liberty.

Today more than any time since Appomattox, America needs *REAL* States' Rights. Americans are helplessly watching as the Federal government spends the United States into countless trillions of dollars of national debt; they are watching as the Federal government continues its attack upon the display of Christian symbols such as the Ten Commandments; they are watching as the Federal government refuses to defend the borders of this country while sending our troops around the world to defend the borders of other nations; they are watching as the Federal government works to expunge traditional moral values from society and they wonder why we can't force the Federal government to abide by the Constitution and respect our traditional moral value system.

The answer to the question of "Why can't we force the Federal government to abide by the Constitution and respect our traditional moral values," cannot be correctly answered as long as one is kowtowing before the icon of

Lincoln. Shortly after the defeat of the South a Radical Abolitionist and Freethinker, Colonel Robert Ingersoll, noted why the War for Southern Independence was pursued so diligently by the party of Lincoln: "The great stumbling block, the great obstruction in Lincoln's way *and in the way of thousands,* was the old doctrine of States' Rights." Thus we see why the red herring of slavery and destroying America is used by the enemies of the South. As long as America continues to kowtow to the enigma of Lincoln, "we the people" of the once sovereign states will never have the tools needed to force big government to abide by the Constitution and respect our traditional moral value system. In other words *REAL* States' Rights will not be a threat to our masters in Washington. This is Lincoln's legacy to America — something most Tea Party Patriots refuse to come to grips with and therefore they are doomed to a continuation of more failure. One thing is for sure; modern day communists, socialists, liberals and secular humanists still hate the "old doctrine of States' Rights" but find much in Lincoln and his love for Federal supremacy to admire.

It is the hope of many that with the republication of Blacknall's work, more Americans will take a look at what Mr. Lincoln did to the original Constitutional Republic of Republics known as these United States of America and help return this nation to the principles of the founding fathers. When America understands Lincoln as the South did in 1860, this nation can then begin to undo the adverse consequences of Appomattox.

Deo Vindice,

Walter D. Kennedy
James R. Kennedy

Introduction

Written almost 100 years ago, *Lincoln As The South Should Know Him* remains a reference source for historians today. It seems Southerners in the early part of the twentieth century faced the same problems and misinformation Southerners in the twenty-first century face. In fact, twenty-first century Southerners face even more problems with the political correctness and liberal agendas of modern day historians — if history is even taught at all.

O. W. Blacknall was a prolific author and a life-long defender of the Confederate cause. He was published in the magazines and newspapers of the day on a variety of issues, from horticulture to the American Revolution and even poetry. But most of his writings were on the War for Southern Independence.

Lincoln As The South Should Know Him, written in 1915, has emerged as his signature work. Not content to only address Lincoln's malfeasances, Blacknall also exposes the atrocities overseen by Generals Sherman and Grant, their so-called troops and most of Lincoln's cabinet members in this short — but to the point — book.

He makes the best case I have seen for calling the late unpleasantness the War for Southern Independence.

To every patriotic Southerner, War for Southern Independence should be a sacred name. It is the name hallowed by the lips of the men who died to make it a reality.

The causes of the War are explained including the issue of slavery … causes you will not read about in today's history books which come down to what all wars are about — money.

I must caution the twenty-first century reader to put Blacknall's views on race and segregation in the proper context. His views were consistent with the time period in which he lived and should not be judged by today's standards. In fact, he was more enlightened on this subject than most of his contemporaries.

Comparing American society and culture to the great civilizations of Europe is a theme throughout this book and a viewpoint not often seen.

Written in 1915 while war was raging across Europe, Blacknall compares the actions taken by the United States against the Confederate States with actions Kaiser Wilhelm II of Germany was using in Europe.

Lincoln As The South Should Know Him holds a unique place in history as one lone voice of reason and logic in a wilderness of misinformation, falsehoods and political correctness.

— Frank B. Powell, III, Editor
Wake Forest, North Carolina
June 2011

In a blaze of burning roof-trees, under clouds of smoke and flame,
Sprang a new word into being, from a stern and dreaded name;
Gaunt and grim and like a specter rose that word before the world,
From a land of bloom and beauty into ruin rudely hurled,
From a people scourged by exile, from a city ostracized,
Pallas-like it sprang to being — and that word is "Shermanized."

— L. Virginia French

LINCOLN, AS THE SOUTH SHOULD KNOW HIM

What thick hides and short memories we Southern folks have, and how inconsistent we are! We call down anathema on the Kaiser's head for the devastation of Belgium; in almost the same breath we raise paeans to Lincoln, who was responsible for the far more causeless and ruthless devastation of the South by Sherman — Sherman, who waged war so atrocious that its very author could find no name on earth to match, but had to go down below to get it. Well might he, with Milton's Satan, say:

"Where I am is hell."

Satan lit its fires in his won breast; Sherman in the desolated homes of war, made widows and orphans.

If Belgium had its Louvain and Antwerp, so also had the South its Columbia, its Atlanta, its Savannah, its Charleston.

Countless Belgium homes have been burned. But there has been nothing like systematic, utter destruction.

The Kaiser, outnumbered, hard beset, the very existence of his country in imminent peril, has increased his slender store of food by robbing Belgium, electing to starve foe rather than friend. *(This was written in January 1915.)* That vengeance, not necessity, prompted the black path that Sherman cut through the South, the evidence is full and damning. On December 18, 1864, General Halleck, Chief of Staff to President Lincoln, and necessarily in close touch with him, writes to Sherman as follows: "Should you capture Charleston, I hope by some accident the place will be destroyed. And if a little salt can be sown on its site, it may prevent the future growth of nullification and secession." Sherman, on the 24th, answers as follows: "I can bear in mind your hint as to Charleston and do not think that 'salt' will be necessary. When I move, the Fifteenth Corps will be on the right of the right wing, and their position will naturally bring them into Charleston first; and if you have watched the history of that corps you will have remarked that they do their work pretty well. The truth is, the whole army is burning with an insatiable desire to wreak vengeance on South Carolina."

One of Wheeler's scouts, observing Sherman's advance, reported that during one night, and from one point, he counted over one hundred burning homes. And as to the looting, a letter written by a Federal officer, and found at Camden, SC, after the army passed, and given in the *Southern Woman's Magazine,* runs as follows: "We have had a glorious time in this State. The chivalry have been stripped of most of their valuables. Gold watches, silver pitchers, cups, spoons, forks, etc., are as common in camp as blackberries. Of rings, earrings, and breastpins I have a quart. I am not joking — I have at least a quart of jewelry for you and the girls, and some A-1 diamond pins and rings among them. Don't show this letter out of the family."

Sherman long denied burning Columbia, in the most solemn manner calling his God to witness as to his truthfulness. When, after the overwhelming evidence that he did burn it was adduced, he unblushingly admitted the fact, and that he had lied on Wade Hampton with the purpose of rendering him unpopular, and thereby weakening his cause.

But a mere lie shines white against the black ground of Sherman's character.

I could pile up a mountain of facts as damning as those given. But what boots it to prove again what too long ago has been proven — that not since Attila, "The Scourge of God," cut his black swath across Europe fifteen hundred years ago has Sherman's "March to the Sea" had its fellow.

The conversion of the Shenandoah region into a waste so complete that, in Sheridan's own words, a crow flying over it would have had to carry his rations — a destruction not only of every vestige of food, of all animals and fowls, but also of every implement that could be used to make or prepare more food, every millstone, wagon, plow, rake, and harrow, down to the flower-hoes of the women, may have been a military necessity, for this lovely valley was, in some measure, the granary of Lee's army.

The necessities of war demanded that Sherman live off the country he traversed. Those elastic necessities may have been stretched to demand that he destroy even the pitiful stint of food that the South had left; that he wrest the last morsel from the mouth of the mother and babe, lest, perchance, some crumb thereof reach and nourish the men at the front. But what necessity of war, except that brand that Sherman fathered and sponsored, demanded that the torch follow the pillager, that every home be burned, and famishing mother and babe be turned out in midwinter to die of cold and exposure?

"But didn't 'Sherman's March' shorten the war; didn't it shake Lee's lines around Petersburg when his men knew that fire and rapine were in their homes?" is sometimes asked. Doubtless. And it might have shaken them all the more had wives and babes been burnt in these homes rather than left to starve in their ruins. It might have been not only more effective but more merciful. But there are abysmal depths of atrocity from which even the "hired assassin" recoils — that is, unless he belongs to the Attila's, Alvas and Shermans. There are rules of civilized warfare, which the soldier in every extremity must observe or else have heaped upon him the execration of mankind.

The whole world shudders at the robbery and partial ruin of only a part of Belgium. Sherman devastated an area nearly twice as great as the whole of Belgium, and devastated it utterly, leaving only blackened chimneys and starving women and children in his wake. That his hell was only some sixty miles wide was owing to no lack of satanic ferocity on his part. It would have been much wider had not Wheeler, with his handful of horse, hung close to Sherman's flanks; with a quick halter for every marauder he caught in the act. Sherman's little finger was heavier than the whole martial fist of the Kaiser. Belgium was a battleground — the largest and fiercest that even blood-soaked Old Mother Earth ever saw. But it took five million men five months to work wreck and ruin. Sherman did it overnight with sixty thousand. The Kaiser found at least a potential sniper in every window; his every step was a battle. Sherman had only a light screen of cavalry to brush aside, and not always even that.

That there was less starvation in Sherman's path than the Kaiser's — though many a high-born Southern lady kept life in her children for the time with the waste corn slobbered from the mouths of the Federal cavalry and artillery horses — was because the South was large and far less densely populated than Belgium, and that the victims sought shelter in the unravaged regions which Wheeler had saved.

Then there is a hideous chapter in this black book that never has and never will be written — so hideous that even the South has been fain to draw over it the curtain of oblivion. I mean the violence that Southern women suffered at the hands of Sherman's ruffians. It is a well-known fact, and by none better known than by military men themselves, that men herded in camps, removed from the restraints of home, rapidly tend to relapse towards barbarism, and that only the iron hand of discipline can hold them in check. Relax that discipline in one respect, sanction the perpetration of one crime, and all crimes, especially the crime against woman, follows as a natural sequence.

No one who lived in or near Sherman's path in Georgia, South Carolina, or even in this State, after the war was over and the troops marching for disbandment in Washington, can lack knowledge of cases that came to light, despite every effort of the hapless victims themselves to hide them. To recall only the cases which abide with me most vividly, that came practically under my own observation, or that I had first-hand knowledge of — the beautiful girl to whose rescue came one of Wheeler's troopers, and who, seized and used as a shield by the ruffian who had abused her, in her agony begged the trooper to shoot through her body and kill him; but by a dexterous movement the brute was killed over her shoulder.

The cottage, with its rose-covered porch, in which lived the young widow and her three daughters, all noted for their beauty and refinement, at whose door a band of Federal troopers drew rein at dusk — the screams and sobs that all the live-long night the neighbors heard, but dared not stir — the tomb-like aspect of the cottage, with no smoke from the chimneys, no sign of life, for days and days afterwards — the deep grave of forgetfulness that the sorrowing neighborhood dug for the whole horrible affair, where it rests this day. The very first offense of a Negro against a white woman that I ever heard of was committed in this neighborhood, in April 1865, by one who had been under Sherman's tutelage. What, indeed, was the saturnalia of crime against Southern woman for a generation afterwards but the aftermath, the legacy, of that foulest blot on American history —Sherman's vaunted "March to the Sea"?

It is a maxim of war, as it is of common sense, that the higher the rank the greater the fame or blame for any given act. In every crime that sprang from this lack of discipline — and no one can question that practically all did so spring — the men higher up, who invited the crime by lowering the bars of discipline, were worse criminals than the perpetrators themselves. Above the perpetrator stood the commander of the army, Sherman; above Sherman stood the commander-in-chief of all the Federal armies, Abraham Lincoln. If Lincoln ever discountenanced Sherman and his methods, he never gave word to it, and he was a man of many words.

George III, whom we were reared to execrate next to Satan, and Lincoln, whom our children are being reared to venerate almost next to God, both sent armies to invade the South, the one in the benighted eighteenth, the other in the enlightened nineteenth century. Surely the charter and conduct of the two commanders put at the head of these invading armies must be some indication of the animus of those two men towards the South. I quote first from Cornwallis's order book, various dates of January, February, and March, 1781, showing him to have been more careful to shield noncombatants from the pettiest theft than Sherman was to save them from the blackest crimes: "It is needless to point out to officers the necessity of preserving the strictest discipline and of preventing the oppressed people from suffering by the hands of those from whom they were taught to look for protection. Lord Cornwallis is highly displeased that several houses have been set on fire today during the march — a disgrace to the army — and he will punish with the utmost severity any person or persons found guilty of committing so disgraceful an outrage. His lordship requests that the commanding officers of the corps will endeavor to find the persons who set fire to the houses this day." "Great complaints have been made of Negroes straggling, plundering, and using violence. No Negroes shall be suffered to carry arms. Provost marshal has orders to shoot on the spot any Negro who may offend against these regulations." "Any officer who looks on and does not do his utmost to prevent shameful marauding will be considered in a more criminal light than the person who committed these scandalous crimes." "A woman having been robbed of a watch, a black silk handkerchief, a gallon of peach brandy, and a shirt, and, by description, by a soldier of the Guard, every man's kit is to be immediately examined." "All foraging parties will give receipts for the supplies taken by them." In some instance two staff officers were actually captured because they had remained behind to pay for supplies requisitioned for the invading army.

"A watch found by the regiment of BOSE. The owner may have same from adjutant on proving property. Immediate inspection of the clothing in possession of the women is to be made. Their clothing to be regularly examined at proper intervals hereafter, and every article found in addition thereto burned at the head of the company. Officers are ordered to make this examination at such times so as to prevent the women (supposed to be the source of this infamous plundering) from evading the purport of the order."

(Sherman's majors general brought their harlots along, loaded them with stolen jewelry, and desecrated Southern homes with them overnight before applying the torch next morning.)

I might quote at great length the British commander's restraining words and cite instances of stronger measures, but will cite only one.

After Cornwallis' virtual defeat at Guilford he retreated to Wilmington, then passed northward through the State on the way to his doom at Yorktown. Even if policy rather than principle had influenced him for, as he well knew, the game was lost. While at Halifax tidings reached him that a woman had suffered at the hands of

Tarleton's troopers forming his advance guard. Taking a bodyguard of only one dragoon, Cornwallis spurred forward and overtook Tarleton near the present town of Garysburg. The whole command was halted till witnesses could be brought up. It was then dismounted, lined up, the two offenders, one a sergeant, identified, tried by drumhead court martial, and strung up to the nearest tree.

So much for the army that the tyrant, George III sent. Eighty-four years later the superman, Lincoln, sent an army along much the same track. The object of both armies was to subdue the invaded region and win it back to their respective governments.

The tyrant of the eighteenth century, as we have seen, sought to subdue by waging honorable warfare against combatants and protecting the person and property of noncombatants.

And the superman? To devastate and utterly ruin every inch of territory that the far-flung wings of his great army could compass, a compass limited only by the activity of the Confederate cavalry on its flanks.

Even then, if in the conflict of the strong North against the weak South such cruel measures were necessary, if the occasion demanded that every Southern woman and child that could be reached be deprived of food, clothing, and shelter, and turned out in midwinter, it does seem that this superman would have sent the sanest and humannest of all his lieutenants to accomplish this fell work — would have tempered wrath with mercy. Instead, he sent Sherman, the demoniac. Charity impels me to dub him only demoniac, possessed of a demon, rather than to believe one of my own species could be demon outright. Listen at his ravings and judge. They are taken at random from his orders and reports, and whole pages could be filled with such venomous utterances:

"As to the Kentucky secessionists, I hope General Burbridge will send them to Dry Tortugas [a sandy island of insufferable heat and glare south of Florida] — men, women, and children — and encourage a new breed."

"Hang a few secessionists now and then."

"I am going into the very bowels of the Confederacy, and propose to leave a trail that will be recognized for fifty years."

"I propose to sally forth to ruin Georgia, and expect to leave a hole that will be hard to mend."

"I am perfecting arrangements to push into Georgia and make desolation everywhere." "I will make Georgia howl."

"Arrest all people, male and female, and let them foot it into Marietta. Let them take their children and clothing, provided they have means of hauling them." (Lacking these means, the only inference is that both were to be left behind.)

"I propose to march, leaving a patch of desolation behind."

"I will see that Atlanta is utterly ruined."

And like master like man. Small wonder that Sherman's underlings filled every item down the long, black list of crime, from plain stealing to arson, rape, and murder. Lack of space forbids that I even classify the fiendishness — from the midnight burning of towns, driving the unprotected women and girls into the streets crowded with unrestrained soldiery, to slipping the quid of tobacco into the pitiful jug of sorghum, which the mother, everything else destroyed, has saved from her blazing home and held desperately to as the last bar between her little brood and actual starvation; the spattering of the little tot with blood as the calf was shot in her arms, she having hugged it tight to save it from the fate of horses, cows, sheep, pigs, and poultry shot down and left to rot around the house.

Decency bars me from more than hinting at the wanton and studied befoulment of precious heirlooms and sacred things before applying the torch, and all the insults and outrages that helpless woman had to endure from brutal man when the clock is set back to primeval savagery.

It is all-sufficing to say that as a rule they did their level best to match with their own black deeds their leader's black words. It would take a pen with the three-league sweep of Kipling's artist's brush in the hereafter to do justice to the breadth and depth of it all — and then no mind could comprehend it all and retain its saneness.

Sherman apologists (I never heard of his having a defender) have cited the liberal terms he offered Johnston and his remonstrance with the Northern politicians as to their treatment of the South after the war as showing that he was not all black. As to the terms offered Johnston, I would say that was all a matter of policy in which motives of humanity might and might not have had a part. As to the other, judging the man by his deeds and knowing his animus towards the politicians. I am forced to suspect that his motives were akin to those that prompted Macaulay's Puritan to condemn bear-baiting — not that it gave pain to the bear but that it gave pleasure to man. Or was it, rather, that like the hyena, having mangled his helpless prey, he was jealous of the jackal pack?

That Lincoln was an able man, of many amiable qualities, is wholly beside the point. The colossal public crimes of history were committed by men altogether amiable, or estimable, or both, in private life. Julius Caesar, the destroyer of ancient liberty, was the most genial and companionable of men. Charles the First, who but for the headsman might have destroyed modern liberty, was a tender-hearted, lovable gentleman of stainless private life, as was Robespierre, who glutted the very guillotine with innocent blood. Who could out-cajole Napoleon or Louis the Fourteenth, arch enemies of mankind, or, as to that, Satan himself?

Did it brighten the lot of the shell-torn inmates of Southern hospitals to know that the maker of medical and surgical supplies, contraband of war, was a man of infinite jest? Were the skeletons rotting in the vermin-encrusted burrows of Andersonville, or freezing in the icy sheds of Point Lookout and Fort Delaware, helped by knowing that the breaker of the cartel could not abide the sight of misery? Did it lessen the sorrow of Southern mothers, who, roof-trees ablaze, fled with their little broods to the wintry woods and swamps, to know that the hand that swayed the besom of hell always rested tenderly on the head of his own children? Did it diminish the agony of Southern maidens, writhing in the clutches of Sherman's licentious soldiery, to remember that the one at the head of it all was a virtuous man?

Lincoln, the public man — the only Lincoln that we knew — was the creature of the Republican Party — the party born of anti-Southernism, anti-Jeffersonism, the innate and truceless foe of individual, local liberty, as opposed to centralism, imperialism.

Did Lincoln ever rise a hair's breadth above his party? Is there a single instance in which he failed to see with its eyes, act with its spirit? When, during the opening, progress, or close of the war, did he display that greatness of mind or of heart, that magnanimity, that should wrest homage from even a vanquished and ruined foe? When or where was he other than the incarnation of Republicanism?

Shall we honor him for the dexterity, not to say duplicity, with which the Peace Commissioners, the able men whom the South sent to Washington in March, 1861, in a strenuous endeavor to avert war, were kept dangling, while in violence to solemn promise the secret expedition was prepared and despatched to reinforce Sumter, a measure so close akin to perfidy that it alarmed and enraged the South and precipitated war?

It has been a platitude of history that the war was inevitable. Like most platitudes, it has very little thought back of it. In exact proportion as we disentangle the skein of past diplomacy and past politics, in the same degree do we discern that few if any wars were inevitable.

In public in no less than in private life the soft answer turneth away wrath. At one touch of a frank, honest, sympathetic hand the most sinister political kaleidoscopes in history have instantly assumed benign combinations.

But that is all by the way. The wisest men of that day did not think war inevitable. Men North and South were working hard for peace.

Lincoln's words and actions made only for war. How different was Washington's action in Shay's rebellion! Not waiting for overtures, he took the initiative and appointed a commission to confer with the malcontents, and thus averted bloodshed.

Shall we honor Lincoln for his emancipation proclamation? The blackest crime laid at the door of George III was that he unleashed a handful of savages against our frontiers. Lincoln, as far as in him lay, unleashed four million savages (which the North held that slavery had converted the Negro into) in our very midst, against our defenseless women and children. To the good feelings existing between the races we chiefly owe that the horrors of St. Domingo, multiplied ten thousand-fold, were not repeated at the South.

Shall we honor him for the flagrant breach of the cartel, and the resulting hells — Point Lookout, Fort Delaware, Johnson Island, Camp Morton, Camp Chase, Rock Island, at the north; Andersonville, Belle Isle, Salisbury at the south, and many more prisons in each Republic?

Shall we honor him for out-Kaisering the Kaiser in making medical and surgical supplies contraband of war, thus adding still lower depths to those hells, as to the whole war, on the Southern side?

Shall we honor him for Sherman's Gargantuan orgy of crime in Georgia and South Carolina, and for the vile dregs of it that our own women had to drain long after the hostilities ceased?

Lincoln's tragic taking off naturally caused a great revulsion of feeling in his favor at the South. This has prompted us to believe that had he lived the Republican lion would have transfigured itself into a lamb the moment that

*"The war drums ceased from throbbing
And the battle flags were furled."*

In other words, that mildness and benignancy quite angelic would have marked the reconstruction period, or rather there would have been no reconstruction period at all, but, instead, a kind of family reunion, with Sewards, Ben Wade, and Thad Stevens *et id* as ecstatic ushers.

But from what act of Lincoln's do we find justification for this belief, or rather hope? There were good words enow. For, statesman as he was, Lincoln was first, last, and always the politician, seeking the public will before the public weal. Not by words, but deeds, must a man be judged. Words are the politician's stock in trade. "Deeds proclaim the man;" words too often hide him. It is true that when Richmond fell he authorized the calling together of the Virginia Legislature. But it was avowedly because he believed that it would recall the Virginia troops from Lee's retreating army, and he wished to give opportunity to do so. The moment that Lee surrendered he withdrew the permit, and ordered the arrest of any members who disobeyed the order to quit Richmond promptly.

It is far more likely than otherwise that Lincoln's death lightened the heel that sought to grind us in the mire. The incarnation of Republicanism in war, there is not a shadow of reason for believing that in peace he could have thwarted the politicians of their prey, though he would no doubt have deprecated their violence.

Why, pray, should he who shut his eyes while 18,000 square miles of Southern homes were being Shermanized, converted into a hell more vast and hideous than even Milton's imagination ever winged, all under plea of military necessity, have been less pliant when, a little later, political necessity called? Are Southern institutions more sacred than Southern women? Does the South set a greater value upon her political welfare than on the lives of her children, the honor of her women?

The Republican politicians were bent upon the utter humiliation and degradation of the South; upon forcing on her civil rights miscegenation, mongrelism. Their animus is shown by the clash with Andy Johnson, the fierce fight against even the stint of justice that a renegade would fain have accorded the land of his birth. So fraught was their attitude to the South with malice prepense that they in a measure overreached themselves, and brought about a partial reaction of feeling among the Northern people at large. Then the scrimmage with Johnson distracted their attention. He got many a blow that would otherwise have fallen on our defenseless head. Under Lincoln, their methods would almost surely have been less violent, but probably far more systematic and insidious. Davis might not have been imprisoned or not so long, or Wirz, the commandant of Andersonville prison, executed. But in all likelihood a more furtive, deadly way would have been found to work our undoing. When thieves fall out honest men thrive, and that is about the only chance they do get to thrive.

The man to whom is really due the gratitude of the South is Grant.

Had he not scotched the plan of the Republicans to punish the Southern military leaders, by threatening to throw up his commission if Lee was arrested, there is no telling, the gates of vengeance once ajar, when they would ever have closed.

Turning from Lincoln the Republican to Lincoln the man. Is the wily, not to say tricky, politician, the reveler in "smutty" jokes, the Southern ideal? Lack we, of our own kith and kind, of our own household of faith, great men who were also great gentlemen? Are we so poor in heroes that we must need pedestal the man who led his sections somewhat bunglingly, it is true, but without ruth or remorse in the onslaught that virtually destroyed ours?

Again, is there anything in the achievement of Lincoln so dazzling that it should blind us to everything else? Is there glory for the strong in overcoming the weak, the many the few? Would we ever have heard of Goliath, Xerxes, Darius, and all their like, had they won? Such immortality that they won is reflected from the foes they faced, weaker but of better mettle.

In years to come the case of the South and the North will be cited as the crowning instance of the tyranny of the pen. The American colonies, equal sisters, finding themselves aggrieved by certain unmotherly measures of the mother country, a mother too far off to harm them greatly, and in fact harming only their pocket, and that slightly, yet made war on her, the author of their being, beat her and set up for themselves, calling high heaven to witness, that "Governments derive their just powers from the consent of the governed."

Now, some malign power had laid upon all, or about all, of these sister colonies a great burden, a great curse (Negro slavery), disguised as a blessing, but upon part of them more heavily than others. The sisters lightly afflicted were able to free themselves of this curse not only without scathe, but with actual profit, by shifting their portion of it upon those sisters sorely afflicted to helplessness.

Then straightway the free sisters, seeing how trammeled and helpless the burdened sisters were, not only robbed their pockets by iniquitous tariff laws which bore heaviest on one section, but, what was infinitely worse, they turned their quacks (the abolitionists) loose on them with their nostrums, defeating all the practical efforts of the burdened sisters to cure themselves. Finally, forced thereto by the instinct of self-preservation, the first law of nature, the burdened sisters, now expanded into a domain larger than the whole at the beginning, and three times as populous, took steps to save themselves, to be rid of the persecuting sisters. But these steps were far more deliberate, more orderly, and far more conciliatory than those taken with the mother country at the Revolution.

With all solemnity, observing every form of law and diplomacy, they declared their independence by withdrawing from the Union, as the persecuting sisters had, under infinitely less provocation, repeatedly threatened to do; and, when driven to the wall, turned and defended this "inalienable right," that "Governments derive their just powers from the consent of the governed," with a courage and devotion that never has been surpassed.

That their appeal to the sword should have been lost is no wonder. The sword has ever been the slave of might.

But that a people who so long withstood the sword of the North should have surrendered so quickly, so cravenly, to its pen, must forever stand the wonder of the world. It will he incredible that an intelligent, high-spirited people, a people showing in every other respect mental and moral fiber of the most robust order, should have been transfigured into such groveling thralls that they not only forswore the high, expressive, and honorable name of the struggle given to their fathers, "The "War for Southern Independence," but came to see only wild political folly, madness, in the sane and heroic endeavors of the fathers to establish and maintain a republic suited to the genius of the Southern people, one in which issues the most portentous that ever faced any people could have been settled by these people themselves and not by the arbitrary and hostile power of an alien people, or rather left unsettled, and in such a posture that, like Banquo's ghost, it would never down.

The compromise name, "War Between the States," which our perhaps overcautious leaders thought best to use while the South still had her head in the lion's mouth, was, as they must have known, a clear misnomer. But a misnomer, a wrong name, they doubtless held, was better than a bad one, better than the name rebellion with all its load of opprobrium and reproach.

Nevertheless, whatever the war was, it was not war between the States. The States, as States, took no part in it, were not even known in it. It was a war between two thoroughly organized governments and for one great principle, that completely overshadowed all others — Southern Independence. To the Northern mind the struggle of the South to reassert the cardinal principle of the Declaration of Independence, that all men are entitled to life, liberty, and the pursuit of happiness, was rebellion; to the Southern mind it was not.

To every patriotic Southerner, War for Southern Independence should be a sacred name. It is the name hallowed by the lips of the men who died to make it a reality.

To all of us, from Jeff Davis and Zeb Vance down to the smallest "shaver" who waved his homemade straw hat to a frazzle as the soldier trains rolled by, it was the "War for Southern Independence" never a war between the states. To the thousands who died that the name might live, who breathed out their gallant lives amid the smoke and dead-fallen air of battle, or who, braver still, starving in Northern prisons, surrendered to the fell Sergeant Death rather than to the wiles of the captor who offered the renegade everything, it was always, everywhere, the War for Southern Independence. They never believed they were dying in a mere squabble between States, but to achieve Southern Independence; to erect a great Southern Republic, under whose golden aegis Southern civilization would flower into the glory and envy of the whole world. It is treason, rank treason, to their memory for us to dub it otherwise.

"What is History But a Lie Agreed Upon?"
— Napoleon

In the first edition of the foregoing part of this brochure I endeavored to reach the Southern people through my usual channel, the Southern press. To my very great astonishment I found it closed to me. Editors who for nearly forty years had met me more than halfway for copy (my pen, since as a young man I gave up a remunerative career as a magazine writer, has been devoted to the defense of the ideals and aspirations of the Old South) now slammed the door in my face. Thus was I driven to appeal to Caesar, to appeal in pamphlet form from the Southern press to the Southern people.

Their response has been most cordial, showing that whatever the Southern press may be, the Southern people themselves are patriotic. But men and women pass; the printed word endures. What the papers are today the people must be tomorrow or the day after.

"But for Lincoln's influence you might not here and now dare to write as freely as you do" is the gist of some of the editorial criticism my paper has met, though it was a layman who expressed it in those words.

I submit that it is high time that the patriotic men and women of this generation register a most emphatic protest against the attitude of a part of the press and people before it is too late.

Did we need just what we got in the sixties, and ought we to be shouting glad we got it?

Shades of the Fathers! We, of the purest strain of the stock that gave freedom to the world; we, from whose very loins sprang the architect, the builder and the defender of American liberty — we, so poor in statecraft, so bankrupt in morality, that an alien must come with three million at his back, and with fire, sword, and rapine save us from ourselves! Yet such is the logical, the inescapable deduction from the premises our children will be taught to accept!

The North, flinging to us the dross of physical prowess and purblind devotion to a fallacious cause, has arrogated to herself the gold of moral rectitude and political infallibility. We have been taught, and are tamely accepting the dictum that the South, when she lost hold on the motherly apron strings, when she foolishly ventured from under the aegis of Northern protection, relapsed swiftly towards despotism and anarchy, and that Appomattox alone saved us from political disintegration!

Is this true? Do we alone deserve the odium of being the one branch of the race too weak to frame civil institutions that could stand the crucible of war? The Romans, the sanest and most practical political people the world has over seen, always when the ship of state was in peril, put a dictator at the helm.

"Inter Arma Leges Silent."

In the clash of arms, law was silent, suspended. Private right, private wrong, had to wait until the foe was vanquished and Rome safe.

Rome, when beset the hardest, never faced the disadvantages, and was rarely ever in the extremity that the Confederacy stood from beginning to end. Never in any land was there direr need that a hand, strong, arbitrary, untrammeled by peace-built law and usage, garnering every man, every resource, should strike as one at the Giant Foe.

Yet was there a dictatorship at the South, or any semblance of one? Did war submerge law? It is a maxim of our race, Free speech, free press, free land. Tyranny ever chains first the tongue, strikes her first blow at the palladium of liberty — free utterance.

Right here in North Carolina the Confederate government had its fullest swing. The State lay nearer to Richmond (and distance, owing to crude transportation facilities, was a far more formidable thing then than now) than any other State as largely free from invasion. It affords a fair instance of the contact of the Confederate Government with the civil life of the people.

Now, living evidence is still abundant that no man was molested for opinion's sake or for word spoken. That the press remained unmuzzled, the files of the *Raleigh Standard*, which to the very end preached stark treason to the Confederacy, stands in everlasting evidence.

Governor Vance of North Carolina and Governor Brown of Georgia, though patriotic men, seeing fit, even in extremity, to place State rights and other considerations before Confederate success, hampered the Confederate executive to a degree never before or since tolerated under such circumstances. It is true that the impressment and conscription measures were grievous burdens, especially here in such close reach; but they were laws of the Congress, and not the fiat of the executive. In short, much of the defensive power of the South was lost by the failure of President Davis to wield the full measure of power that would readily have been acquiesced in by the people at large. Never, not even in the great crises, did Jefferson Davis exercise one-tenth the dominance over the Confederate Congress that Woodrow Wilson now does over the Federal. Davis's decrease of popularity towards the end came from no abuse of power on his part, but mainly from the stigma which the world attaches to failure — that is, except in case of the soldier. Around him war flings a saving halo.

Let us glance at the other side of the picture — at the status of the civilian of the North. The Federal government, infinitely superior in resources, had not the same urgent need for unity. Yet we find its actions immeasurably more arbitrary than those of the Confederate government. Not under the old regime in France were *lettres de cachet* as plentiful or more potent. It was a well-known boast of Stanton, Secretary of War, that he could touch a bell on his table and order the instant arrest of any man in the Union. Fort McHenry at Baltimore, Fort LaFayette at New York, Fort Warren in Boston Harbor, and the old Capitol Prison at Washington, became veritable bastilles, crammed with political prisoners, men immured for what they had said or for what it was suspected they might say or do. In the old Capitol Prison, at least, executions were frequent.

Never imposed Fate a heavier burden on any people than on the South when she was made the ladder on which the benighted African must climb civilization and Christianity. Not the opprobrium, but the profound sympathy of the whole world, and especially of the Negro himself, is our just due; for never, since time began, has a race climbed from darkness to light so swiftly and at so small a price to itself — at such fearful cost to the instrument of its elevation.

As is well known, slavery was no Southern indigene; no plant that grew here only. It was only the inheritance of the ages. Sanctioned by immemorial and universal usage, and even by Holy Writ itself, it was indeed the very oldest of all human institutions. Founded originally, in part at least, upon morality, upon the pity which spared instead of slaying the captive, it thus became the bedrock of all civilization. But slavery in this land, and at that date, was a thing strangely out of place and out of time. So much so, indeed, that one wonders as to Fate's motive in the misplacement. Did a spirit of impish irony impel her, or was she actuated by a deeper motive, when she dropped this Old World estray, this foundling in the cradle of liberty, the New World — the motive that as we

"Broadened with the act of Freedom "

we should also

"Grow strong beneath the weight of duty"?

Slavery would surely have gone, even had Lincoln never been born. The drift of the world had set against it, deep and resistless. Harking back two thousand years to Epictetus, it had come to see that not to him who getteth, but to him who doeth a wrong, cometh the chief harm. Emancipation was inevitable, and to hold that the Southern people, the purest-blooded branch of the sane and virile Anglo-Saxon race, the race which gave liberty to the world, and which in all lands and under all conditions had stood for justice and fair play, as it came to see it — for us to hold that this, our branch, would have been so degenerate, so recreant to the genius and spirit of the stock, so inferior to its forbears, or even to the "lesser breeds" to the south of us that did put it by, that it lacked the manhood to free itself from the incubus of slavery, is a worse slander than even our foes would dare put upon us.

It is argued, and by our own writers as well as others, that the slaveholding class dominated the South, and that self-interest, cupidity, would always have impelled this class to block emancipation. I would reply that slavery in divers forms was long an institution with our race; but that the race in its progress put it by, despite the strenuous opposition of the slave-holding class — as it must have done in this case. The whole moral trend of the race rendered any other course impossible. The fact that medieval serf was white and strong, and the modern slave black and weak, would undoubtedly have made the work of emancipation harder; but the race is morally stronger now than then.

There is one fact generally overlooked, which would have added greatly to the practicability of emancipation. That was the fact that the slave- holding classes at the South were in a minority of about six to one. Every reform, social or political, that our race has achieved has been in the face of a wealthy minority far stronger than that. In fact, it is almost a truism of our politics that the people, as opposed to aristocracy, always win in the long run. No civilization has survived in which this rule did not hold. The chief reason that the dust covers so many of the splendid civilizations of the past was because the great mass of the people remained inert to the end. The broadening of the franchise right here in North Carolina in the fifties, whereby the aristocratic dominance of the State Senate was abolished, is significant proof of what the middle-class manhood of that generation were capable of.

One thing is certain: Had the Negro remained in our midst the South would have avoided the irretrievable error of the North in making the slave a citizen first and a man afterwards. As emancipation would have been gradual, so also would have been the elevation of the freedom. As he attained the full stature of manhood, so he must perforce have been invested with the rights and privileges of a man. But he hardly would have remained. Colonization being impracticable at that late period, segregation would probably have been the solution of the race problem. Even in this sanctimonious age we exclude the Asiatic. Where would have been the sin in settling the African in a prescribed area of the country, and excluding him from the other parts of it? Compared with the Yellow peril, the Black peril is Olympus to a wart.

Some degrees of wrong and injustice there might have been. Wrong and injustice are not often absent from the affairs of this world. But who is bold enough to assert that the measure of them could have equaled, or even distantly approached, that infinitude of injustice and of wrong — the orgy of political madness — reconstruction, whose blighting effect was to distract and stunt, perhaps forever, the development of the Negro, and to sow, as fast as the hand of malice could sow, the very salt of annihilation over the civilization and life of the South?

As is well known, the emancipation movement in its earlier, saner stages had its warmest and ablest supporters at the South. Washington, Jefferson, Henry, Madison, and the foremost men of that time sought earnestly for some practicable method of putting an end to slavery, which was generally regarded as a curse, and especially so to the whites. But for the perfectly natural reaction caused by the rabid, incendiary methods of the abolitionists, which, beginning about 1830, flowered so quickly and hideously in the Nat Turner butchery of white women and children, gradual emancipation would soon have been under way, and would almost surely have ended slavery with that century. I would not deny that the development of cotton growing caused by the perfection of the cotton gin, and the resulting enormous increase in slave values, would have made emancipation a tremendous problem. But sphinxes — political, social, industrial, moral, religious, racial — had lined the pathway of our race down the ages. All had been answered, and, we believe, answered right, by the communities which had most at stake.

To our branch alone was denied the priceless boon of answering for themselves the most momentous problem of them all, a problem that involves not only our prosperity but our very existence, and which now can only deepen and darken with the passage of the centuries. Were our immediate forbears — the men whose courage and heroism in war placed the Lost Cause in fame's eternal keeping, whose fortitude and sagacity triumphed even over reconstruction, who hurled back the envenomed dart, Negro suffrage, upon the heads that sent it — weaklings, men whose destiny was safer in the hands of an alien and hostile section than in their own? Perish thought so blasphemous!

How few of us, too, have ever analyzed the famous Emancipation Proclamation; have ever tried to ascertain the proportions of politics, diplomacy, and philanthropy couched therein ; have ever regarded its true purport and bearings. Did it free, or seek to free, all the slaves in the land ? Oh, no! Only a part. What part? Those in the hands of Lincoln's enemies. Those within the Union lines, those in the hands of friends, were not affected by the proclamation. They remained in bondage so far as this instrument was concerned. Lincoln had been dead nearly a year before total abolition was legally brought about. Outside of the punitive intent, the prime motive of the proclamation was, first, to buttress the Republican Party against the rising tide of Democracy; second, the Union arms against those of the Confederacy. The military end sought was to weaken his enemies by destroying their property.

Naturally, he struck at their chief asset — their slaves. If he had been able thereby to destroy any or all of other kinds of their property he would have done so. If his simple mandate would have cut the throat of every work animal, milk cow, fire every roof-tree, and imperiled the honor of every woman in the South, there is no reason to believe that he would have withheld its utterance; for it was his word that sent hundreds of thousands through the South to do these very things.

If we must accept subjugation, even of mind and of spirit; if we must view the whole bloody drama through the eyes of our enemies; if we must believe that the blow came from above and not below; that we not only richly deserved but sadly needed just what we got — then the right men to honor are the pioneer abolitionists, Garrison, Wendell Phillips, Gerrit Smith, and men of that feather. They boldly stood for abolition, when to stand meant hatred, contempt, and imminent peril of life and limb. These men had no ulterior motives. They breasted the tide of fortune. Lincoln floated upon it. If honor we must the sowers of the wind whose fearful whirlwind we had to reap, let's honor these, the real heroes of the cataclysm. True, they sent John Brown pikes to butcher us with; but they were perfectly willing to be butchered themselves in the same cause.

No one would deny that Lincoln was an enemy of slavery. He was a product of a class and of an environment that drew in hatred of slavery and of slave-holders with every breath. Moreover, most thinking people, North and South, were enemies of slavery in theory. With Lincoln and the North it was only a theory. With the South it was a fact, a grim fact which, foisted upon us by English and later by Northern greed, time had now riveted upon us. The growth was cancerous.

But would you go to your butcher to remove even a cancer?

Emancipation at the time, and in the manner in which Lincoln sought to enforce it, was a politico-military measure, and nothing else. 1862 was election year. Lincoln, great man and statesman as he undoubtedly was, was also politician to the core. And when did your politician, big or little, ever fail to trim his sails to the wind — to save the party and then let the party save everything else? Federal arms had sustained such repeated and disastrous defeats that Northern opinion was turning to the Democratic Party, which favored peace. Defeat stared Republicanism in the face. Something must be done to stem the tide. The emancipation proclamation was the answer. While primarily a political move, great things were also expected of it in a military way. It was largely believed that the slaves would rise and deal with Southern women in a way that would cause the Southern armies to crumble in a day, as each man rushed home to save his own.

As a military measure it was the fiasco of the ages. Not a slave stirred or lifted hand. But its political effect was immense. It instantly brought into the Republican camp every cohort of abolitionism, and held all in line to the end, though these lines bent fearfully under Jackson's blows at Chancellorsville, and again, when soon after the grey columns surged northward to Gettysburg, and even when, much later still, Grant's army recoiled in temporary paralysis from the futile assaults on Lee in the Wilderness.

Still, this is not an attack on Lincoln, nor do I seek to revive sectionalism, further than consistency and self-respect demand. I am well aware that patriotism is a matter of geography. That all depends upon the side of the line on which you were born, But so, also, is renegadeism. High moral law demands that we be true to our fellows, our surroundings. The Washingtons and Lees obeyed it. The Arnolds and Iscariots defied it. This is simply an earnest protest against accepting as a Southern hero, a Southern exemplar, a man, no matter how worthy personally, who was a leader of Northernism, and of Northernism in its attitude of implacable hostility to the South and Southern ideals. It is natural that the Negro should honor Lincoln. He gave the Negro freedom. And the North, he gave the North dominion over the South. He carried out Northern ideals of centralism, imperialism. The Southern ideal, State rights, home rule, the palladium the world over of the weak, met destruction at his hands. With glaring inconsistency, we still hold the ideal to be true, while paying homage to the chief instrument of its destruction.

"Suppose the South had won? What then?" is the common query, usually in tones of utter deprecation. I would reply that had the South lost; what then? The blackest page in the annals of our race! Would the Lees, the Davises, the Hamptons, the Vances, the Grahams, the Ashes, the Grimeses, the Clarks, the Jarvises, the Hills, the Carrs, the Ransoms, the Averys, have been less fit to deal with even the tremendous issues left by war than the Sewards, the Wades, the Stevenses, the Holdens, the Tourgees, the Deweeses, the Cuffees, who fumbled them till, with an effort that paralyzed all other endeavors for a generation, we wrenched the helm from their hand.

The War of 1861, notwithstanding the unfortunate slavery complication, was as much a war of liberty as that of 1775, or that of 1642 in the Mother country. It was a struggle for local self-government against centralism and all the evils that have skulked in its shadow, monopoly, trusts, extortion in its protean guises. A quicker exploitation of our resources — and a quicker destruction — has undoubtedly ensued. But where has the wealth gone? Would not those resources be safer in the hands of nature than in the hands that now hold and use them as a lever to oppress and extort?

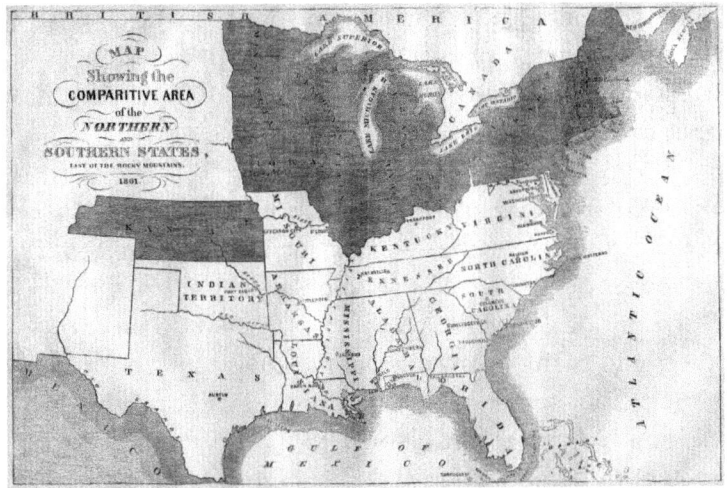

The war, waged for State rights, for local self-government, the principle for which the flower of our manhood laid down their lives, was the half-conscious effort of our branch of the race — the branch that events have proven to have had the keenest political instincts of all — to avert this torrent of evils; some then plainly disclosed to our clear vision, some even now just emerging from the haze of the days to be.

Then circumstances and heredity had made the South the citadel of conservatism. What a brake on the wild wheels of this mad world her conservatism must have been could it only have won the prestige of success, had it only been its luck to be backed by the stronger battalions of heavier guns! In all human probability it would have saved us from many of the evils above indicated, as well as the maze of fads, follies, and isms in which we now grope in such utter bewilderment.

Even Southern writers have to stultify themselves every time they approach the subject as to what might have been if the victory had been accorded to us instead of our foes.

Loud in praise of the statesmanship of the old South, strong in the belief of the justice of her anise; yet no sooner do they reach the point where the stronger battalions of the North prevail than they drop on their knees and thank Heaven for having saved the South from herself. They thank Providence that instead of giving the South a respite from Northern incendiarism, instead of smoothing her way so that she might put by slavery in the least harmful manner, it brought down upon her three millions of armed men, who, destroying the flower of her manhood, breaking the heart of her womanhood, consigning her children to poverty and ignorance, reducing her people to virtual beggars, and would have forced miscegenation, mongrelism, upon her but for the mettle of her stock! Others may think as they will, but I cannot bring myself to hold any such slanderous opinions of Providence. I cannot see the hand of Providence (though I might a sootier one) in such fell work as, on the one hand suffering Northern abolition, incendiarism, to arouse and inflame the resentment of the South, and, on the other hand, Northern ingenuity to invent the cotton gin, thus at the critical moment infinitely increasing the value of slaves, and forestalling the South in her earnest endeavors to put an end to slavery. That the South was denied the inestimable privilege of abolishing this curse which the cruel hand of Fate had fastened upon her, thus saving herself the unspeakable loss and woe and humiliation that the war entailed, is no proof that the

Southern way was the wrong way. Success is no proof of right, nor failure of wrong. Yet men whose very religion is founded on faith in One who from the low viewpoint of material things sounded the abysmal depths of failure, now cry aloud that it is. The vessel of iron will ever smash the one of gold against which in the rough mischances of the world it is thrown, though the latter, from the fineness of its material and the nobleness of its design, might be fit to edify mankind forever.

O. W. Blacknall.
Kittrell, NC, January 1915

(In regard to race and segregation, I would add that the question was extensively discussed at the North in the early part of the war, and Florida suggested as the State to be thus utilized when the South should be subjugated. This being considered too small, Texas was proposed.)

O. W. Blacknall

Store clerk, farmer, tobacco manufacturer, strawberry expert, naturalist, nurseryman and prolific author — Oscar Williams Blacknall was a remarkable man who met with a tragic ending.

A native of Kittrell, NC, in Vance County, Blacknall's family first settled in the area when it was still a part of Granville County before the Revolution. His great-grandfather served with George Washington, while his father was colonel of Company G, 23rd Regiment NC Troops during the War for Southern Independence. Colonel Blacknall led his men at Yorktown, Williamsburg, Seven Pines, Chancellorsville and Gettysburg until mortally wounded early on September 19, 1864, near Winchester, VA, and died on November 6, 1864, when young Oscar was ten years old.

His father's death in service to the Confederacy had a profound effect on the rest of Blacknall's life and left him with intense pride in the Southern cause. First published in 1915, *Lincoln As The South Should Know Him* is an excellent example of his Southern sentiments and remains a reference for historians today. Plus, it was said his collection of books and artifacts on the Confederacy was immense.

But to focus solely on his Southern writing would do him a grave disservice because he was much, much more. Blacknall wrote a lot of poetry which was published in popular magazines of the day. The poem on the next page was published in the *North Carolina University Magazine* October 1894.

The Mocking Bird

O mocking-bird that since the flowing mist
    Of spring enameled quickening woods and lea
    Hadst sung, informing both with melody,
Why now thine erring vocal flight desist?
Thou found the amplest summer day, I wist,
    By far too short thy couch, the star-gilt tree,
Thou Shakespeare of all birds, ennobling plagiarist,
    Not all the glory that on sky and leaf
Finds transient home, and gems thy throne as yet
Was never hard-wrought throne begemmed can set
    At large thy prisoned song; but brimmed with grief
Thy soulful eyes gaze out in mute alarm
At rude unthatching winds that work thy lair harm.

                                          O. W. BLACKNALL

Blacknall's letters and articles were also widely published in newspapers and periodicals across the country on a variety of subjects and topics. Strawberries were his life's work and he wrote extensively about cultivating and growing strawberries. He published a major work in 1902, *Practical Strawberry and General Berry Fruit Culture also of Grapes, Asparagus, Rhubarb, Etc.*, 124 pages covering all aspects of raising strawberries successfully. In addition, he published a monthly paper, the *Strawberry Specialist*, 16 pages for 50¢ a year. His Continental Plant Company nursery in Kittrell sold plants to growers across the United States and strawberry plants all over the world. At the time it was one of the largest nurseries in the world. He also served as vice president of the North Carolina Horticultural Society during this period.

Even though he was admired and respected in the community, not all was roses for he suffered a nervous breakdown at the age of 36 and was never well physically after that. His first-born son, also named Oscar, died young, early in his promising career. Several years later two other sons and a married daughter were struck by various maladies. Events in Europe were pulling the United States closer and closer to world war which brought the prospect of his only other son being called to service came to be too much for him to handle.

On the afternoon of July 6, 1918, O. W. Blacknall calmly shot his wife Carrie at the dinner table, shot his other daughter Kate in the backyard, after she ran out of the house, and then he killed himself. Blacknall was almost 66 years old at the time of his death. The community was shocked and saddened by this tragedy. The three were buried at the Kittrell Cemetery in a wide grave with three caskets, the father in the middle.

One of his friends and admirers, T. T. Hicks, concluded his account of Blacknall's life in the local newspaper with "Our Father knows that Oscar Blacknall had the treasure of the Spirit, though in an earthen vessel."

— *FBP III*

CHARACTERS
FLOY KATE LANDERS
REUBEN LANDERS
OLETA
SHERIFF TROTTER
MIZ ARNETTE

SETTING
A farmhouse kitchen in remote Hardesty, Oklahoma

TIME

Act One
Scene 1: October, 1934,
Scene 2: One week later
Scene 3: Late that same night

Act Two
Scene 1: A few days later
Scene 2: Later that same day

MUSIC USE NOTE

Licensees are solely responsible for obtaining formal written permission from copyright owners to use copyrighted music in the performance of this play and are strongly cautioned to do so. If no such permission is obtained by the licensee, then the licensee must use only original music that the licensee owns and controls. Licensees are solely responsible and liable for all music clearances and shall indemnify the copyright owners of the play(s) and their licensing agent, Samuel French, against any costs, expenses, losses and liabilities arising from the use of music by licensees. Please contact the appropriate music licensing authority in your territory for the rights to any incidental music.

IMPORTANT BILLING AND CREDIT REQUIREMENTS

If you have obtained performance rights to this title, please refer to your licensing agreement for important billing and credit requirements.

THE MYSTERY OF MIZ ARNETTE was first produced by One Thirty Productions, in Dallas, Texas in May 2011. The performance was directed by Marty Van Kleeck, with sets and costumes by Marty Van Kleeck, lighting by Jaymes Gregory, and sound by Graeme Bice. The cast was as follows:

FLOY KATE LANDERS	Zoe Kerr
REUBEN LANDERS	Sonny Franks
OLETA	Gene Raye Price
SHERIFF TROTTER	R. Bruce Elliott
MIZ ARNETTE	Cindee Mayfield

ACT ONE

Scene One

(As the house opens and the audience enters, the whine and howl of wind is relentless until the lights go down.)

(The wind dies down a bit.)

FLOY KATE (VOICE OVER). The grass was stirrup-high. No trees. Daddy said you could see a man coming on horseback from here to the Gulf of Mexico. No one could sneak up on us. But elements from the sky and earth snuck up on us, leaving us caught between, in their clash. The winds twisted away the earth, blowing our outside world to dust. But inside, an equally ferocious storm hovered like a huge cloud, threatening to destroy us.

(The wind crescendos. The lights fade to black.)

(The wind starts to die down again as the lights come up to reveal the kitchen of a farmhouse in Hardesty – a remote town in the Oklahoma Panhandle. It is October, 1934.)

(The walls and floor of the kitchen are plank. It is a single-sided house, the external and internal walls being one and the same, a portion of which is covered with newspaper comic strip pages.)

(There is a door with a screen door upstage center. Upstage left, there is a door leading into two shotgun bedrooms. Upstage right, next to the outside door, is a pantry, its entrance hung with a quilt. A window is left of the outside door. Stage right is a door leading to **REUBEN**'s *bedroom.)*

(A kitchen table and five chairs occupy the area stage right. Stage left is a dry sink cabinet. Downstage of it is a large bucket of water with a dipper. Upstage of it is an iron stove. A few pots and pans and a skillet are hung on nails on the wall.)

*(**FLOY KATE** enters from the upstage [outside] door, a bandana around her face to shield her from the wind. She is a small, thin, freckled, fourteen year-old girl with her hair in pigtails. She lights a kerosene lamp. She takes a rag and wipes off the oilcloth on the table and chair seats. She continues to wipe dust off every surface in the kitchen as her father, **REUBEN**, enters.)*

*(**REUBEN**, wearing coveralls and a jacket, is 45. He is tall, rangy, and weathered.)*

(He beats his hat off on the door, and wipes his face and neck. A train whistle blows in the distance.)

*(**FLOY KATE** sets a pan of water and washrags on the table. They wipe themselves down.)*

REUBEN. That dirt was black. Must have been half of Kansas in that storm.

FLOY KATE. At least it wasn't that awful gray New Mexico dust.

REUBEN. But still and all, wasn't as bad as it could have been.

FLOY KATE. Those dumb chickens.

REUBEN. Did any of them blow away?

FLOY KATE. I got them all under the house except one chick. What about Ol' Worthless?

REUBEN. Didn't have any trouble with him. 'Course that mule's smart. Headed right for the barn. 'Course that barn, it's not much good cover what with all the dust coming in them slats.

FLOY KATE. At least he's in out of the wind.

REUBEN. Oleta could have pitched in and made a hand.

FLOY KATE. Should we ask that of her? She's a paying boarder.

REUBEN. You suppose she slept right through the storm?

FLOY KATE. I imagine. It's only three o'clock in the afternoon. But, well, she does work late.

REUBEN. She usually runs for the storm cellar, but it's pert near filled up with dust now.

FLOY KATE. We're lucky this house is tight. We've ridden out a lot worse.

REUBEN. Probably be better off if the whole place just blowed away.

FLOY KATE. We can't give up, Daddy. Where'll we go?

REUBEN. California, like everybody else.

FLOY KATE. If I could just find me another job. But since the café closed down, what else is there?

REUBEN. You got a job, little lady. You keep workin' on that essay of yours. You're gonna win that essay contest.

FLOY KATE. But we need the money now. And since the cafe closed down, what else is there? Oleta's got the only job left at the beer joint.

RUBEN. The beer joint'll be the last place to close.

FLOY KATE. Daddy, I'd hate to do it, but I guess we could always sell the mule.

REUBEN. That's a jackass of an idea, girl. Nobody'd want Ol' Worthless. Besides, that money won't stand between us and the poor farm.

FLOY KATE. At least you've got a job, Daddy.

REUBEN. A job I hate.

FLOY KATE. You're lucky to have one, Daddy. Somebody's got to do it.

REUBEN. But, delivering bank foreclosures? On my neighbors?

(A car pulls up outside.)

FLOY KATE. *(looking out the window)* Sheriff Trotter drove through that storm!

REUBEN. I dread every time I see him coming.

FLOY KATE. It'd be easier, Daddy, if every time you see him coming, you think of the money.

REUBEN. Maybe he's just come to see Oleta this time.

(**FLOY KATE** *opens the door and* **SHERIFF TROTTER** *enters carrying a bundle of magazines and comic books.*)

(**TROT** *is portly and around 50. He wears an Oklahoma sheriff's uniform with a cowboy hat, boots, and coat.*)

FLOY KATE. Come on in, Sheriff Trotter. Light and set.

REUBEN. Did you drive through that storm?

TROT. I was caught about halfway here. I pulled into the barn over at the old Johnson place, waited it out. It peeled the roof right off Flint Henderson's place.

REUBEN. We better strike out and see if we can make a hand.

TROT. They're gone. Left for California four days ago.

(puts stack of magazines on table)

Today's your lucky day. Conductor Mills threw a whole big bunch of magazines off the train for you this morning. "Modern Screen," "Unsolved Mysteries," "Reader's Digest."

(giving **FLOY KATE** *the comic books)*

Must have been a bunch of kids on the train. Look at all these funny books.

FLOY KATE. I'll put them aside for Oleta. Would you like some coffee?

TROT. Don't mind if I do.

My main reason for coming is I just got a call that Pretty Boy Floyd robbed a bank up in Ohio some place called East Lambertville and they say he's headed this way so I'm out giving warning. The last thing we want is for a family to be held hostage and have to engage in a shootout.

RUEBEN. But he'd head for Hell's Fringe over there in the Cookson Hills where he was raised and still has family.

TROT. He's too smart for that. He knows that's the first place the law would look for him.

RUEBEN. But why would he come here?

TROT. To hole up. It's isolated and a train comes though here.

RUBEN. Is he traveling alone?

TROT. He usually doesn't, but the gang may have split up.

REUBEN. I hope that's all the bad news you come to drop off.

TROT. Sorry, nope. Got a notice for the McCubbins for you to deliver.

(He pulls an envelope out of his shirt pocket and hands it to **REUBEN.***)*

REUBEN. This is the third foreclosure this month.

TROT. Think of it this way. It's more money for you every time you deliver one.

(We hear **OLETA***'s voice trilling offstage, singing a popular song of the day.)*

FLOY KATE. *(to* **TROT***)* I figured she'd get up when she heard you was here.

OLETA. *(calling)* Is that who I think it is out there?

*(***OLETA*** enters, buttoning up her dress. In her 40s, she is a blowsy peroxide blonde, tending toward fleshiness.)*

Why, hello, Sheriff Trotter.

FLOY KATE. We sure could have used some help during the storm, Oleta. Where was you? In bed?

OLETA. Under the bed.

TROT. I'm out giving warning that Pretty Boy Floyd may be headed this way.

OLETA. Pretty Boy Floyd's headed this way?

TROT. There's a $23,000 bounty on his head.

OLETA. I wouldn't mind running into Pretty Boy Floyd, especially for that kind of reward money.

(**OLETA** *pours herself a cup of coffee and spoons in three spoonfuls of sugar.*)

TROT. You don't need all that sugar.

OLETA. *(as she licks spoon and drops it into the suger bowl then sits beside him)* You mean I'm sweet enough already?

TROT. Sweet enough to make your teeth ache.

OLETA. Oh, go on now. You're just pulling my leg.

(**TROT** *whispers something to her. They giggle and she pinches his cheek. They exchange a look.*)

(spying the magazines) What have we got here? "Modern Screen." Doesn't Ginger Rogers look beautiful! I love her hair. And did you bring a – oh, here it is – "True Confessions!" And "Ace Detective Stories!"

REUBEN. *(reading a newspaper)* Let's see what Will Rogers has to say in his column. "The way to solve the traffic problem is that the only cars that should be allowed on the road are those that are paid for."

(They all chuckle.)

TROT. Ain't that the truth. Well, I expect it's time I got back to putting out the word about Pretty Boy Floyd. Reuben, I'll give you a ride. I've just got to drop Oleta off at the beer joint.

OLETA. Thank you, Trot. Oh, by the way, Floy Kate, my room's covered in dust.

FLOY KATE. I'll get to it.

OLETA. Thanks, girl.

FLOY KATE. But first I've got to work on my essay for the contest.

(**TROT** *and* **OLETA** *exit.* **REUBEN** *puts his arms around her.*)

REUBEN. Your mama would be so proud of you writing this essay. She had so many hopes and dreams for your future. I'll be back by suppertime. See you directly.

(He exits upstage center.)

(**FLOY KATE** *rinses out the coffee cups. She goes off into her bedroom and brings back a Big Chief tablet and stub-end pencil. She puts it on the table, opens it, reads a few words to herself. She bends over the page, erases something, and makes a correction. She stands and starts to read aloud.*)

FLOY KATE. Essay contest sponsored by the National Benevolent and Protective Order of Elks. The Land Where I Live, by Floy Kate Landers. Oklahoma means Land of the Red Man. But on the old maps, it was called the Great American Desert. But I do not live on a desert. I live on a plain.

(*A figure [***MIZ ARNETTE***] appears in the doorway in silhoutte – .*)

From all over the country, people made a mad dash into the Indian Nation to stake a claim. On April 22, 1889, my grandfather made The Run in a buckboard wagon hitched to a matched team of fine bay Morgan horses. It was quite a sight. People came on foot, on bicycles, on horseback, muleback, and in surreys. After riding over hill and dale, the flat grasslands looked appealing to the original settlers.

MIZ ARNETTE. Dangling participle!

(**FLOY KATE** *whirls around terrified.*)

FLOY KATE. What?

MIZ ARNETTE. A dangling participle!

(*beat*)

FLOY KATE. Who are you? Are you part of the Pretty Boy Floyd Gang?

MIZ ARNETTE. Indeed not! If I threw in with a gang, it wouldn't be Pretty Boy Floyd's.

FLOY KATE. (*a sigh of relief*) Thank Heavens!

MIZ ARNETTE. It might be with Baby Face Nelson. May I come in out of this inclement weather?

FLOY KATE. Oh well, ma'am, I –

MIZ ARNETTE. Please, lest I be blown away like the Witch of the West Wind?

FLOY KATE. Oh. Oh, I'm sorry.

(She opens the door. **MIZ ARNETTE** *steps in carrying a valise and a wicker suitcase.)*

*(***MIZ ARNETTE** *wears an opera cape and a hat with a veil held on by a jeweled pin. She wears gloves, tan cotton stockings, and black oxfords with a slight heel. While her clothes are worn, she has a certain chic style and elegance all her own.)*

(She never takes off the following pieces of jewelry: a very long pearl necklace or a chain with a gold medallion, single-drop large pearl earrings, wide gold slave bracelets on each wrist, and rings on every finger and a small dagger in a jeweled sheath hanging from her belt.)

MIZ ARNETTE. It's fortunate you're not far from the rail station. I'm weary unto death tramping through such a dreary landscape after my long train ride. As I was saying, a dangling participle is a misplaced modifier describing a word other than the word intended. What you have erroneously written is that your grasslands are riding on horseback.

(to the speechless **FLOY KATE***)* I am Miz Arnette. *(lifting her veil)*

(silence)

And you are?

FLOY KATE. Floy Kate Landers.

MIZ ARNETTE. Floy. Obviously a Latin derivative of Florence. Meaning "to flower," "to bloom." And Kate from the Greek Katherine meaning "pure." An innocent flower struggling to bloom in this arid, desolate place.

FLOY KATE. Where did you come from?

MIZ ARNETTE. The question is not where did I come from. The question is where am I going. Always stay in the affirmative. Look to the future. I've come about the room.

FLOY KATE. What room?

MIZ ARNETTE. Why, the room you advertised.

FLOY KATE. What?

MIZ ARNETTE. I've got it right here.

(producing a newspaper clipping)

"Room to rent. Landers farm. House just west of the rail station with a yellow windmill. Hardesty, Oklahoma." So, like Don Quixote, I looked for the windmill.

FLOY KATE. *(taking the clipping)* But that was four months ago.

MIZ ARNETTE. Oh, surely not.

FLOY KATE. Yes, look here. June 23, 1934. It's October now. The room has been taken.

MIZ ARNETTE. *(pushing through)* What about this room?

FLOY KATE. That's just a storeroom. Nothing would fit in there but a little pallet.

MIZ ARNETTE. Eureka! I prefer a small, enclosed hiding space. I've spent many a time camping out. In tents, igloos, teepees. All over the world in all climes.

FLOY KATE. I wouldn't feel right charging you for that. I suppose I could give you my room.

MIZ ARNETTE. That would be less invasive.

*(**FLOY KATE** crosses the kitchen and opens the door into her room. **MIZ ARNETTE** peers in.)*

So you live here alone?

FLOY KATE. My daddy, my mamma died.

MIZ ARNETTE. I'm sorry to hear that. Semi-orphaned.

FLOY KATE. It's only us. Not a lot of folks come this way.

MIZ ARNETTE. So you're free from spying eyes and tattling tongues.

FLOY KATE. But we do have a boarder, Oleta.

MIZ ARNETTE. The one who took my room?

FLOY KATE. Yes, ma'am.

MIZ ARNETTE. And what does Oleta do?

FLOY KATE. She runs the beer joint.

MIZ ARNETTE. Ah. Quenching the thirst of the weary wandering wayfarer. But I would think that would not be an easy job in a dry state.

FLOY KATE. It's only three point two beer, and we don't get many wayfarers.

MIZ ARNETTE. *(murmers to herself)* Perfect.

MIZ ARNETTE. So Oleta has to come through here to get out?

FLOY KATE. I'm afraid so.

MIZ ARNETTE. Oh, dear. This does complicate things. You must inform her to respect my privacy and make her entrances and exits quickly and quietly.

FLOY KATE. Here, I'll get your grip.

(**FLOY KATE** *picks up* **MIZ ARNETTE***'s suitcase.*)

MIZ ARNETTE. Oh, yes, my portmanteau.

(**FLOY KATE** *gets a kerosene lamp and goes into the bedroom.*)

FLOY KATE. *(from off)* I'll just collect a few of my things.

MIZ ARNETTE. We have yet to settle on the rate.

FLOY KATE. It'll be five dollars a week.

MIZ ARNETTE. What does this price include? Does it include board? How many meals?

(**FLOY KATE** *comes out with an armful of her things and puts them in the alcove.*)

FLOY KATE. Breakfast and supper and that's a dollar extra.

MIZ ARNETTE. I don't eat breakfast so it should be fifty cents. But I will take a cup of strong black coffee in the morning.

FLOY KATE. I'm sorry; I'd have to get the full amount.

MIZ ARNETTE. That seems unreasonable.

FLOY KATE. That's the rate.

MIZ ARNETTE. I won't quibble. I'll pay you sixty cents.

FLOY KATE. I'll take seventy-five.

MIZ ARNETTE. Very well, but I want two cups of coffee. Black and very strong.

FLOY KATE. You don't take nothing in it?

MIZ ARNETTE. No, I don't take ANYTHING in it. Now, here are my requirements. If you would, please keep this table cleared so that I can spread out my work here. Also, it's necessary that I get my mail in a timely fashion, so you must be sure to go to the post office every day.

FLOY KATE. But we don't go every day.

MIZ ARNETTE. It's crucial that I get my mail. I'm expecting money orders, addressed to Cryptic Critiques. So, I have to have it to pay you.

FLOY KATE. I'll take a week's advance.

MIZ ARNETTE. Oh, no, I can't until I get these money orders. You'll have to wait on that.

FLOY KATE. But I'm going to need cash.

MIZ ARNETTE. We'll settle that later. I can no longer discuss finances. Right now, I'm utterly exhausted and my nerves are raw from my travels. I must lie down with my feet up and a cold cloth on my head.

(She picks up the wicker suitcase and goes into her room, stopping in the doorway.)

What time is supper served?

FLOY KATE. Six o'clock.

MIZ ARNETTE. Please call me five minutes before you're ready to sit down.

*(**MIZ ARNETTE** closes the door. **FLOY KATE** stands there, looking after her in amazement. She goes to the table and picks up her writing tablet.)*

FLOY KATE. What did she call that? A danged parsnip..le?

*(From **MIZ ARNETTE**'s room comes a high, piercing shriek.)*

(At the same moment, the kerosene lamp on the kitchen table goes out, leaving the stage in darkness.)

(A long beat.)

*(**MIZ ARNETTE** comes out of her room carrying a lit kerosene lamp. The light reveals **FLOY KATE** standing in the middle of the kitchen, a skillet raised above her head.)*

MIZ ARNETTE. No, no, don't be frightened. I should have explained. There are two of us.

FLOY KATE. Two of you?

MIZ ARNETTE. Myself and Little Lucifer.

FLOY KATE. What's a Little Lucifer?

MIZ ARNETTE. My traveling companion. We've been together for years.

FLOY KATE. What is it?

MIZ ARNETTE. He's a tamarin.

FLOY KATE. A tamarin?

MIZ ARNETTE. Yes. Of the family callithricidae. A tiny monkey of the hurdy-gurdy species. He's a stimulating and enjoyable companion.

FLOY KATE. Does it bite?

MIZ ARNETTE. Not unless crossed.

(Another shriek comes from the bedroom.)

FLOY KATE. How am I ever going to explain this to Daddy?

(blackout)

Scene Two

(A week later. A haunting train whistle in the distance.)

(MIZ ARNETTE is working at the kitchen table. She has papers spread out all over it. She has exchanged her black oxfords for a pair of worn Chinese scuffs.)

(FLOY KATE is trying to set the table around MIZ ARNETTE's clutter. She stands over her with forks and plates.)

MIZ ARNETTE. Just one moment. I need to look up something in Deuteronomy.

FLOY KATE. What exactly are you writing?

MIZ ARNETTE. I'm rewriting the Bible.

FLOY KATE. How long have you been at this?

MIZ ARNETTE. Twenty years. It needs elaborating.

FLOY KATE. Why?

MIZ ARNETTE. In those days, they were writing on scrolls, so they had to conserve space. There are a myriad of unresolved mysteries that need to be researched.

FLOY KATE. What are you going to do with it?

MIZ ARNETTE. My work is sought out by Biblical scholars all over the world, many of whom I met in my travels to lands of ancient cultures. But, alas, brilliance and creativity are not always rewarded. Many a time, people have sought to suppress my work. There are no bars on the mind. It cannot be confined. Of course, it can be a lonely life. But fortunately I have Little Lucifer.

(OLETA enters from the bedroom carrying a stack of magazines.)

OLETA. Can't you keep that durn monkey quiet?

MIZ ARNETTE. He's expressing himself.

OLETA. *(yelling back into the bedroom)* He never shuts up!

(setting the magazines next to the other stacks in the kitchen)

MIZ ARNETTE. I noticed you moved Little Lucifer's cage and put it next to the window. That is not your province. He must never be near the window. His lungs will fill up with dust.

OLETA. If we're lucky.

FLOY KATE. Can monkeys get dust consumption?

OLETA. You're just here under sufferance. Reuben would never have allowed you to move in, for sure not with that nasty monkey, if Floy Kate hadn't pled your case. And if they hadn't needed the money.

MIZ ARNETTE. I've noticed some of my other things moved as well. Please do not touch any of my belongings.

OLETA. You're hallucinating. Who'd want to? You don't have nothing anybody would want.

(**OLETA** *sits at the table, pushing aside some of* **MIZ ARNETTE***'s papers.*)

MIZ ARNETTE. Please don't touch my work!

(**REUBEN** *comes in from outside. As he beats his hat on the door,* **MIZ ARNETTE** *gathers her papers from the table.*)

REUBEN. Ain't nothin' in the rain register but six inches of dust and a dead June bug.

MIZ ARNETTE. "Where is the Lord that led us through a land of deserts and drought, and of the shadow of death?" Jeremiah 2:6.

(**MIZ ARNETTE** *takes her papers into her room.*)

OLETA. I saved the newspapers for you, Reuben. I knew you'd want to read Will Rogers.

REUBEN. Let's see what he has to say in this one. "I don't belong to any organized political party. I'm a Democrat."

(*He chuckles.*)

FLOY KATE. (*handing* **REUBEN** *a wet rag*) Daddy, wash up. We're about ready to sit down. I hope there's not too much grit in this food.

(*knocking on* **MIZ ARNETTE***'s door*)

Miz Arnette? Time for supper.

(**MIZ ARNETTE** *comes back in sits at the table across from* **OLETA**.)

(Little Lucifer lets out a little shriek in the bedroom.)

OLETA. Floy Kate, your daddy didn't figure on taking on any livestock. Did you, Reuben?

REUBEN. That's for sure. *(reaching in his pocket)* Miz Arnette, I found something that might interest you out on the north edge of the property.

MIZ ARNETTE. Oh, it's shaped like a flower. What is it?

REUBEN. It's a rose rock. There's a formation of them out there. They're red because of all the iron in them. And every one of them petals is a crystal. They form in circles and that's what makes them look like a rose. I've seen them big as your hand.

MIZ ARNETTE. I've traveled the world looking for the miracles of nature and now I'm holding one in my hand right here in the Oklahoma panhandle.

REUBEN. And the wind keeps uncovering them with every storm. All different kinds of rocks and fossils. Who knows how long they've been buried? This country's filled with nature's wonders.

(The sound of a car pulling up outside.)

And they've got those White Sands over in New Mexico. I wonder about them, if they're still there or if they've been blowed away.

OLETA. *(at the window)* It's Sheriff Trotter.

(**MIZ ARNETTE**'s *antenna goes up.*)

(**OLETA** *stands up, turns away from the table, to straighten her skirt and blouse. She quickly reaches under her skirt to pull her blouse down. She pulls up her bra strap.*)

MIZ ARNETTE. A sheriff? He's coming here?

REUBEN. Yes, ma'am. He drops by from time to time to do business.

MIZ ARNETTE. To do business?

REUBEN. And to see Oleta.

MIZ ARNETTE. *(hastening toward her room)* Ah, forgive me. I don't want to intrude if you are having guests.

REUBEN. No, no. You are not intruding. Sheriff Trotter would find you very interesting.

(**MIZ ARNETTE** *is caught.*)

TROT. *(at the door)* Hello, the house!

REUBEN. Come in, set a spell.

FLOY KATE. *(getting up)* Here, let me get you a plate.

TROT. Thanks anyway. I've already eat supper.

FLOY KATE. Well, let me give you a cup of coffee.

TROT. I'll take you up on that.

REUBEN. Sherriff Trotter, this is our new boarder, Miz Arnette.

TROT. Miz Arnette.

MIZ ARNETTE. *(all charm and bravado)* Enchantee.

TROT. Come again?

MIZ ARNETTE. How do you do? Well, I feel so much safer knowing a man like you is in charge with Pretty Boy Floyd's gang on the loose.

TROT. I've dealt with my share of criminals and felons.

MIZ ARNETTE. Tell me, how do you treat your felons?

(*This scene is flirtatious and teasing.*)

TROT. Depends on what they are charged with. But this county's got a hanging judge. I can read people pretty good, sometimes get a confession.

MIZ ARNETTE. And have you been able to read me so quickly?

TROT. Right off the bat. You're easy to read.

MIZ ARNETTE. *(warily)* Really? And of what do you find me guilty?

TROT. You're a thief!

MIZ ARNETTE. Oh, really? I assure you, I am carrying no contraband.

(She stands holding her arms wide.)

You may search me if you like.

TROT. What you have stolen is the most precious thing a man has to give.

MIZ ARNETTE. What's that?

TROT. His heart.

MIZ ARNETTE. I confess.

OLETA. That must have been some time back!

MIZ ARNETTE. True, but aren't I lucky, the statute of limitations has run out.

FLOY KATE. *(giving him a cup of coffee)* Here you go.

*(**TROT** sits down next to **OLETA**.)*

TROT. How you doing, girl?

OLETA. Perked up since you come in.

TROT. Lookin' mighty pretty today.

OLETA. Got on my marrin' lipstisk

TROT. So, what brings you to Hardesty, Miz Arnette?

MIZ ARNETTE. I need a place where I can have some solitude and concentrate on my work.

TROT. What work is that?

MIZ ARNETTE. I'm rewriting the Bible. Old Testament only.

TROT. *(after a beat)* Rewriting the Bible? How do you go about doing that?

MIZ ARNETTE. Currently I'm expanding the story of Samson and the harlot.

FLOY KATE. Delilah?

MIZ ARNETTE. Exactly.

OLETA. Everybody knows that story.

MIZ ARNETTE. They only think they do. They don't know all of it. I have been able to ascertain many more details.

FLOY KATE. Like what?

MIZ ARNETTE. For example, beginning with his birth. An angel appeared and said he'd be blessed by God as long as he didn't shave or cut his hair or drink any alcoholic beverages.

OLETA. The best Burma-Shave sign I ever seen –
"Whiskers long
Made Samson strong,
But Samson's gal
She done him wrong.
Burma Shave"

MIZ ARNETTE. The Philistines are upon us.
But what people don't know is Delilah wasn't his first lustful temptation. He was on his way to propose to another woman whose name remains lost to the ages – but which I am working on uncovering – when he was attacked on the road by a vicious Asiatic lion, which he had the power to smite due to his long hair and abstinence. Then several days later, on his way to be married, he passed by the lion he had killed. He was taken aback to note that bees had built an enormous beehive within the carcass. A repellent sight, to be sure. Nevertheless, prior to the nuptials, he devised a riddle for his thirty groomsmen which went thusly: "Out of the eater, something to eat. Out of the strong, something sweet." Well, the thirty groomsmen became enraged by the riddle. They told his bride if she didn't find out the answer, they'd set fire to her and to her father. So using her feminine wiles and charms on the wedding night, she seduced the answer out of Samson. The next morning, when the groomsmen answered the riddle correctly, it was Samson's turn to be enraged. He forthwith gave the bride to the best man and said, "Fine. You can take her to feed and house." Then he tied torches to the tails of three hundred foxes and set them loose in the streets of the town, thus ending his initial betrayal by a woman – whose name I am trying to locate.

OLETA. Three hundred fox tail? Sounds like a tall tale to me.

TROT. That story sounds like you're stretching the blanket.

MIZ ARNETTE. I assure you I do not prevaricate. Read your Bible. Judges 14 through 16. It's all there.

TROT. Well, what happened next?

MIZ ARNETTE. Samson meets Delilah at a babbling brook. He's enamored by her, but what he doesn't know is that she's a spy working for the Philistines.

TROT. Oh, like Mata Hari.

MIZ ARNETTE. Precisely. She has a duplicitous purpose behind her assignation, which is to trick him into revealing the secret of his strength. Samson disports with her seductively, and teasingly tells her he will lose his strength if he is tied with new rope. While he is asleep, Delilah binds him. Upon waking, to her astonishment, he snaps himself free of her fetters. "Tell me the secret of your strength," she asks him again and again. Eventually, Samson is blinded by his lust and his better judgment eludes him. Like many a man before him.

OLETA. Maybe he just got sick of her nagging him.

MIZ ARNETTE. *(ignoring her)* He reveals to Delilah that he will lose his strength and power if he is shorn of his locks. That night, as he lies sleeping, Delilah does just that. When he awakes, he is blinded, tortured, and imprisoned.

OLETA. And bald.

MIZ ARNETTE. But during his tortures and travails, his hair grows out and his strength returns. He smites the iniquitous Philistines with the jawbone of an ass and pulls down the temple, killing all of them and himself.

FLOY KATE. But what about Delilah?

MIZ ARNETTE. Whereabouts unknown.

TROT. A missing person.

MIZ ARNETTE. She's one of the world's greatest unsolved mysteries. I've been on the trail of her disappearance for many years.

TROT. You sure tell a good Bible story. I'm pleased to have met you, Miz Arnette. Good luck on your detective work.

(getting up)

Reuben, I have a reason for coming out here.

REUBEN. You don't have to have a reason. We're glad to see you anytime. Just come on by.

TROT. This time, you're not going to be glad to see me.

REUBEN. Why's that?

TROT. This is hard to tell you, Reuben. Grievous hard. I sure hate to be the one to tell you.

(**FLOY KATE** *turns away and starts to cry as* **TROT** *hands* **REUBEN** *a foreclosure notice.*)

FLOY KATE. *(crying)* Oh Daddy!

REUBEN. It ain't your fault.

(**FLOY KATE** *goes to* **REUBEN** *and puts her head on his shoulder.*)

(**REUBEN** *puts his arms around her.*)

TROT. *(at the door)* I'm awful sorry.

(*As* **TROT** *leaves,* **OLETA** *heads to the window.* **MIZ ARNETTE** *and* **OLETA** *wordlessly exit to their rooms.*)

RUBEN. There, there, we can try to figure something out. Talk about this tomorrow.

(*He kisses her on the forehead. They exit,* **FLOY KATE** *to the pantry,* **REUBEN** *to his room. Silence. The lights dim. Pause.* **MIZ ARNETTE** *peers out of her room; all clear. She moves silently to the dry sink, reaches to the shelf over sink and takes a whetstone. She removes the dagger from its sheath dangling from her waist and starts to sharpen it as the lights fade and the wind rises.*)

(blackout)

(curtain)

Scene Three

(Late at night. The only light onstage is the kerosene lamp on the kitchen table. **FLOY KATE** *and* **MIZ ARNETTE** *sit across from each other.* **FLOY KATE** *is darning socks and* **MIZ ARNETTE** *is mending a tiny coat.)*

(Little Lucifer's swallowtail coat is old, worn, maroon velvet, with the nap worn down in many places. It has epaulets and it is decorated with fringe and braid and gold coins. It is lined in ticking. **MIZ ARNETTE** *is working on the trim. She is smoking a Turkish cigarette in a long holder, and blows smoke rings.)*

FLOY KATE. I'm so scared about those bank robbers coming this way. They say they are headed into Kansas.

MIZ ARNETT. As the saying goes, "The law is an ass." You have nothing to fear. Pretty Boy Floyd and his gang won't go into Kansas; they'll go south into Old Mexico.

FLOY KATE. How can you be so sure?

MIZ ARNETT. Trust me on this. Little Lucifer is so hard on his clothes. But it's difficult for me to be angry with him because he's so smart. Monkeys are as smart as children until the age of five. Then they stall out. I feel that Little Lucifer, however, is at least six or seven.

FLOY KATE. Where did you get him?

MIZ ARNETTE. In a marketplace. Captured in a forest deep in Bahia, Brazil.

*(***FLOY KATE*** goes off to the alcove that is now her room. She comes back with a little box. She takes a little photograph out of it and hands it to* **MIZ ARNETTE**.*)*

FLOY KATE. The furthest I've ever been was visiting my mama's people in Quanah, Texas. Here's a picture of me and my three boy cousins when I was six. They joshed me the whole time I was there because I believed in fairies.

MIZ ARNETTE. Well, I believe in fairies. One only has to see the exquisite drawings by Arthur Rackham of Titania, Queen of the Fairies, or to have witnessed the actress Maud Adams in Peter Pan, or hear Mercutio's speech about Queen Mab.

FLOY KATE. Who's Queen Mab?

MIZ ARNETTE. "She is the fairies' midwife, and she comes
In shape no bigger than an agate-stone
On the fore-finger of an alderman,
Drawn with a team of little atomies
Athwart men's noses as they lie asleep;
Her wagon-spokes made of long spinners' legs,
The cover of the wings of grasshoppers,
The traces of the smallest spider's web,
The collars of the moonshine's watery beams,
Her whip of cricket's bone; the lash of film;
Her waggoner a small grey-coated gnat,
Not half so big as a round little worm
Prick'd from the lazy finger of a maid:
Her chariot is an empty hazel-nut – "
Etc…Etc…
Romeo and Juliet, Act I, Scene 4. Now which side of the family were these boy cousins on?

FLOY KATE. Mama's. Here's a picture of her. They say I favor her. She died when I was born.

MIZ ARNETTE. What a sorrow. I believe you do favor her. Such a pretty young woman.

FLOY KATE. And these are my teensy little rose rocks. *(pouring jacks out of a little sack)* And my jacks. And this is a genuine mother-of-pearl necklace. It was my mama's. The clasp is silver. See here. In real tiny lettering. "Silver plate."

MIZ ARNETTE. She would be so proud of you, Floy Kate.

*(**FLOY KATE** pulls out a little snap purse.)*

FLOY KATE. And this is my purse where I kept my tip money when I worked at the café before it closed down. I was hoping to save up some money for college. And this is my Shirley Temple paper doll. I don't play with her no more.

MIZ ARNETTE. ANY more. If you're going to be a writer, Floy Kate, you have to be able to articulate the King's English correctly.

FLOY KATE. Yes, ma'am. When the Yankees came through in Mississippi, my grandfather hid his ten dollar gold piece in the baby's didy. When my grandfather made the Run into Oklahoma, he sewed it in his waistband. President Roosevelt ruled gold had to be turned in but Papa won't do it.

(MIZ ARNETTE handles and studies the gold piece intensely before putting it back in the box.)

MIZ ARNETTE. My dear, how is your essay progressing?

FLOY KATE. Oh, Miz Arnette. I'm stuck.

MIZ ARNETTE. Perhaps you're suffering a little writer's block. It happens to all authors.

FLOY KATE. I don't know what comes next.

MIZ ARNETTE. Read me what you've just written, dear. Let me see if I can help you.

(FLOY KATE gets her essay from her alcove. She stands at the head of the table and reads aloud.)

FLOY KATE. "The Land Where I Live. I was born and have been raised in what thousands of years ago was called the Permian Basin. The land was entirely covered by the sea. It's hard to believe now because the land is blowing away and there hasn't been no rain here for five years. This has been devastating for all living things. The only bird's nest I have seen for over a year was a crow's nest made out of barbed wire."

MIZ ARNETTE. The only thing wrong is your grammar. Once again, the correct phrasing would be "There hasn't been any rain here." But it's very, very interesting.

FLOY KATE. I just hope I win because of the cash prize. I need to give the money to Daddy.

MIZ ARNETTE. Oh, no, dear. That's very admirable, your desire to help. But any money you earn from your labors must be spent on your education. I want to encourage you to realize that at your age the whole world is waiting for you. "A man's reach should exceed his grasp, or what's a heaven for?" Robert Browning. Your opportunities are boundless. Put no limits on your future. You can be anything, go anywhere.

FLOY KATE. Where did you go to school?

MIZ ARNETTE. The world was my school. I am an autodidact, from the Greek root "auto" meaning "self" and "didact" meaning "teacher." Ergo, self-taught.

FLOY KATE. But where were you at my age?

MIZ ARNETTE. Ah, the question is where wasn't I? My father was a wanderer, an adventurer seeking new horizons. We traveled like vagabonds. Forever on the move.

FLOY KATE. To where?

MIZ ARNETTE. The world over.

(She cuts the thead with the knife she takes out of the sheath at her waist and then gestures with the knife in her hand.)

To lands of ancient cultures. To the far-flung reaches of the Earth.

FLOY KATE. But how did you live?

MIZ ARNETTE. Precariously at times. *(returning the knife to its sheath)* For, you see, my father was also a mystic. Like William Blake.

"Tyger! Tyger! Burning bright,
In the forests of the night,
What immortal hand or eye
Could frame thy fearful symmetry?

When the stars threw down their spears,
And watered heaven with their tears,

Did he smile his work to see?
Did he who made the Lamb, make thee?"

He was an explorer. He recovered gold coins from sunken pirate ships. Unearthed opals in Australia, excavated rubies in Burma, emeralds in Colombia, pearls in the mysterious East, and gold nuggets in deepest darkest Africa. When he would strike these treasures, we would live richer than Croesus.

FLOY KATE. What happened to all this treasure?

MIZ ARNETTE. Ah, that is the mystery. Lost to the ages. Except for my slave bracelets and jeweled dagger, gifts from an exotic lover who introduced me to dangerous passions. You see, sometimes my father would leave me in the care of various people. Once a family of Chinese acrobats. I can still walk on my hands. When I was slightly older than you, at the time, my father left me in a Bedouin camp. At first I was fearful of the whole way of life, the tents, having to eat with my hands. The Arabian horses, although beautiful, were unruly stallions. Then slowly I began to adjust. I loved the strong sweet bitter coffee. The hours of indolence lying on piles of carpets shaded by the brightly colored tents. The chieftain was young, maybe thirty five. He had a son about my age at the time. Except for the father's mustache, they were the mirror image of each other. Which to choose? Why did I have to choose? Well, the father being the most experienced of the two, I, of course, succumbed to his seduction. *(sotto voce)* The sweet odor of tobacco and incense that perfumed his mustache, his callused hands, strong from working with his stallions. Lying in the arms of a turbaned sheikh lost in the dreamy smoke of hashish. Heavenly!

(**REUBEN** *enters, startling them.*)

REUBEN. It's awful late for you girls to still be up.

MIZ ARNETTE. *(collects herself; gathering her things)* Yes, it's time to retire. Floy Kate, we'll start again tomorrow. You're progressing nicely.

FLOY KATE. Oh, Miz Arnette, thank you so much. I appreciate you helping me.

(Outside, the sound of a car pulling up, accompanied by the loud laughter of a group of men. The engine keeps running, the car door slams, the car drives away.)

MIZ ARNETTE. Ah, the merrymakers. The revelers have arrived.

REUBEN. Sounds like Oleta's home.

MIZ ARNETTE. I hope I can get some sleep tonight.

*(**MIZ ARNETTE** retreats into her room as **OLETA** comes in the front door, her hands full of newspapers and magazines.)*

OLETA. Well, what are you folks doing up at this hour?

REUBEN. Got a lot on my mind. Couldn't sleep.

FLOY KATE. Miz Arnette and I have been visiting.

OLETA. *(rolling her eyes)* Miz Arnette.

REUBEN. *(to **FLOY KATE**)* Little Bit, you better run along to bed.

FLOY KATE. *(giving him a kiss)* Good night, Daddy.

*(As **FLOY KATE** exits to alcove, **OLETA** flops into a chair at the kitchen table and lolls back with a magazine.)*

OLETA. Ooh, "Photoplay," "Unsolved Mysteries." This is a good bunch.

*(sliding some across the table to **REUBEN**)*

Here's "Liberty," "Redbook," a "Tulsa Tribune" and "A True Dective."

REUBEN. Thank you.

OLETA. *(reading the "unsolved mysteries")* This one's packed full! If Pretty Boy Floyd bein' loose weren't scary enough, they've got the latest about Machine Gun Kelly's gang and the Urschel Kidnapping. It says they took Mr. Urschel right off his screened-in porch in Oklahoma City. Him and his wife were playing bridge with another couple and he was right in the middle of a grand slam. Busted in there, held them at gunpoint, and stripped Mrs. Urschel of a big old diamond ring and a set of sapphire clips. "J. Edgar Hoover has vowed to track Machine Gun Kelly to earth and recover both the money and Mr. Charles Urschel alive."

REUBEN. *(his head in the newspaper)* I see they rounded up a bunch of bootleggers down there in Little Dixie. Again. LeFlore County's always been working alive with bootleggers, yellow-dog Democrats and foot-washing Baptists. Will Rogers said it best.

OLETA. How's that?

REUBEN. Oklahomans will vote dry as long as they can stagger to the polls.

(A long beat as they silently turn pages, lost in their reading.)

OLETA. Reuben! Listen to this!

(sotto voce) Wanted. At large. Suspected of grand larceny. Be on the lookout for white female, approximate age fifty-five. Escapee en route to Terrell Asylum for the Insane. Warning: could be a danger to herself and others. Oklahoma, Kansas, New Mexico, Texas: be on the alert. Family offers large reward.

*(**OLETA** looks up at **REUBEN**. She repeats it.)*

Family offers large reward.

*(They look at each other as the lights go down. The last glow of light onstage illuminates **FLOY KATE**, standing in the doorway, listening to everything they've said as the wind rises.)*

End of Act One

ACT TWO

Scene One

(**FLOY KATE** *is sitting at the kitchen table, writing out her essay. She is copying it from her stack of ragged notes onto clean paper.*)

(**MIZ ARNETTE** *comes out of her room, on her way to the outside door.*)

MIZ ARNETTE. Have you completed your essay?

FLOY KATE. I'm just about there, Miz Arnette. I'm having a few problems. And I have to get it out today.

MIZ ARNETTE. I assure you your problems cannot compare with mine. I, too, am having trouble with my writing.

FLOY KATE. What kind of trouble?

MIZ ARNETTE. I'm working on a story about Solomon from the Apocrypha.

FLOY KATE. What's the Apocrypha?

MIZ ARNETTE. Fourteen books of questionable Biblical merit. King Solomon is giving me a real problem. You've heard pride goeth before the fall.

FLOY KATE. How's that?

MIZ ARNETTE. King Solomon had a flying carpet that could whisk him from Damascus to Medina in just a day. Even today's locomotives can't move that fast. It was an amazing carpet. But disaster struck.

FLOY KATE. How?

MIZ ARNETTE. On one trip, he exhibited pride.

FLOY KATE. Pride about what?

MIZ ARNETTE. That's one of the things I'm stuck on. But when King Solomon exhibited his pride, it caused a horrendous calamity. As the carpet was en route at what must have been the speed of light, King Solomon's men fell off it to their death below.

FLOY KATE. How many men?

MIZ ARNETTE. Forty thousand. And once King Solomon passed an ant hill while journeying and had a conversation with the ants. The Bible is particularly entomophilous. Like Samson and the bees. "And the magicians did with their enchantments bring forth lice upon man and upon beast." Exodus 8:18.

FLOY KATE. What's ento-mor-?

MIZ ARNETTE. The study of insects! "That which the palmerworm hath left hath the locust eaten; and that which the locust hath left hath the cankerworm eaten; and that which the cankerworm hath left hath the caterpillar eaten." Joel 1:4.

FLOY KATE. Bugs in the Bible?

MIZ ARNETTE. The Bible is crawling with them.

FLOY KATE. Your ring! You're wearing a bug!

(They both laugh.)

MIZ ARNETTE. True, a fly, caught in amber for all time.

FLOY KATE. Where did you get it?

MIZ ARNETTE. Therein lies a tale.

FLOY KATE. Oh, tell, tell.

MIZ ARNETTE. Well, my father sent me to the frozen tundra, the far most reaches of Siberia, to negotiate for sables. The sables in this country compared to the Siberian sables had a paucity of hair; too thin, hence, not as luxurious. His idea was to start a breeding farm in Canada, but in the translation, either by mistake or design we had been tricked. Something crucial was missing – the females. The Russians sent only males. But we hoped all was not lost if we could breed them to the Canadian females. But, alas, the Russian males wouldn't go near them, considering them their inferiors. So, since I was stuck in Mother Russia, I decided to investigate the amber market. I traveled by troika to St. Petersburg. I found a ring that charmed me, a tiny creature encapsulated in honey amber. As I took out my rubles to buy it, the jeweler said, "Madame, the gentleman has already paid for your ring." The gentleman? I looked around to see a man leaning against a pillar, dressed in a uniform, trimmed in braid and epaulettes; dangerously handsome, magnetic. He approached, and took my hand. Brushing his lips against it, he said, "Mademoiselle." All the White Russians spoke French, "Like this tiny creature is forever sealed in the amber, I want to forever seal the beauty of you at this moment in my mind's eye."

FLOY KATE. How did you feel when he said that to you?

MIZ ARNETTE. Faint!

FLOY KATE. What happened next?

MIZ ARNETTE. I was introduced into a phantasmagorical world. Nights at the Bolshoi Ballet, a box at the opera, and dizzying nights racing in the horse-drawn sleigh, the snow crackling under its weight, covered in furs, and sometimes little else, kept warm by our passions. If another man even glanced in my direction, he became enraged. Several times I feared a duel. He gave me a tiny gun, a ladies gun, with a mother of pearl grip. So protective, a dear gesture.

FLOY KATE. You were in love with him?

MIZ ARNETTE. Deeply. But alas, it was not meant to be.

FLOY KATE. Why not?

MIZ ARNETTE. He vanished.

FLOY KATE. Oh, no! Where did he go?

MIZ ARNETTE. I know not. My suspicion has always been that he was connected in some way to the Romanoffs and met their same fate at the hands of the Bolsheviks.

FLOY KATE. Your life is filled with so many interesting facts. All I have to tell about is the things the wind has uncovered – the rose rocks and the arrowheads and the dinosaur bones.

MIZ ARNETTE. I find all that very interesting. Some of your antiquities are as ancient as the ones I've been exposed to.

FLOY KATE. But will the judges find it interesting?

MIZ ARNETTE. I assure you I'M much more erudite than these so-called judges.

FLOY KATE. But Miz Arnette, not all people's lives are interesting like yours.

MIZ ARNETTE. Au contraire. Your life is very singular.

FLOY KATE. But your father was an explorer.

MIZ ARNETTE. True. He had the wanderlust.

FLOY KATE. You got to travel with him when he found all these precious treasure and artifacts. In exotic lands. What happened to them?

MIZ ARNETTE. You must never repeat anything I tell you.

FLOY KATE. What?

MIZ ARNETTE. This is to the grave.

FLOY KATE. Oh, no ma'am. I wouldn't never. But I got to tell you. They get to conjecturing, you are not who you say you are.

MIZ ARNETTE. What a preposterous assumption! Jealousy! "The green-eyed monster that doth mock the meat it feeds on." I have experienced all the thrills that life has to offer; ridden the crest of the wave; skipped the high wire without a net. Why would I trade that to be someone else!? So why would they conjecture that?

FLOY KATE. Because you don't have no family

MIZ ARNETTE. Oh, my family. My greedy, avaricious family would have loved to have gotten their hands on those jewels, but, alas, they are lost to the ages. They pursue me like the Furies.

FLOY KATE. The Furies?

MIZ ARNETTE. Hideous snake-haired monsters in Greek mythology. They pursued what they considered to be unpunished criminals. They consisted of Alecto, the Fury of Unceasingness – like my second cousin once removed, a tinhorn gambler – Magaera, the Fury of Grudging – my cousin's wife, a dope fiend addicted to Lydia Pinkham's Patent Medicine – and Tisiphone, the Fury of Avenging – another cousin, a lunatic, a complete madman, an alchemist who believes he's Rumpelstiltskin. Now, that's my family. The scourge of the earth. They are dead to me.

(**OLETA** *comes tearing out of the bedroom, furious.*)

OLETA. Can't you keep that durned monkey corralled? He spilled face powder all over my chiffaerobe and scrawled lipstick on my counterpane.

MIZ ARNETTE. Perhaps he was only searching for my things you have taken from my room.

OLETA. You got nothing I want.

MIZ ARNETTE. I assume you've been through everything to come to that conclusion.

OLETA. You're a scary crazy woman and dangerous, and I should turn you in.

MIZ ARNETTE. On what charge, pray tell?

OLETA. You know what I'm talking about.

MIZ ARNETTE. So, I'm right, you have been through my things. I noticed my sable muff had been moved.

OLETA. Where you keep your gun? Why are you packing heat?

MIZ ARNETTE. I'm a woman alone in the world.

OLETA. I'm goin' to report you.

MIZ ARNETTE. That would be ill-advised. I wouldn't do that if I were you.

OLETA. And why not?

MIZ ARNETTE. Because if you do, I will make your life a living hell.

OLETA. You're crazier than I thought. You don't have nothing over me.

MIZ ARNETTE. Do you think I don't know that you're selling something stronger than three point two beer?

OLETA. Trot wouldn't care if I was doing a little bootleggin' on the side.

MIZ ARNETTE. Maybe not, but the federal agents would.

OLETA. *(For the first time we see **OLETA** scared, sputtering.)* You-You, just better stay away from Trot. I've got dibbies. He's mine. Him and me are thick.

MIZ ARNETTE. You are the victim of an overactive imagination run amok. You have nothing to fear from me in the Eros department. I have no interest in your sheriff or any sheriff.

OLETA. You just better watch it!

(She exits, slamming the door behind her.)

MIZ ARNETTE. Another Fury pursuing me! Now, before the wind comes up too badly again, I'm going out to search for more of your antiquities. I found what I believe to be a dinosaur tooth yesterday. Remember, I want to hear the end of your essay. Don't mail it before I get back.

FLOY KATE. No, ma'am, I won't.

*(**MIZ ARNETTE** puts on her cape and goes out the door.)*

*(**FLOY KATE** leans over her essay, concentrating and copying. She starts to look up a word in the dictionary, when the never-ending wind starts to kick up outside again.)*

(She takes a few spoonfuls of flour and mixes it in a bowl with some water to make a paste. She tears some comic pages from a newspaper and rubs them with the paste. She takes the pages and applies them to the wall, sealing it against the dust.)

(As she works, she whistles "Way Down Yonder".)

*(**REUBEN** comes in from outside.)*

FLOY KATE. Daddy, there's a big ol' chink that's opened up here in this wall.

REUBEN. Well, it's a single-wall house.

FLOY KATE. Is there a storm coming?

REUBEN. Not yet. But you can count on one coming along directly. Where's Miz Arnette?

FLOY KATE. She's gone out on one of her foraging trips for more artifacts.

REUBEN. When do you expect she'll be back?

FLOY KATE. You never know.

REUBEN. She's an odd one alright.

FLOY KATE. Like a person from another world.

REUBEN. What do the two of you talk about so late at night?

FLOY KATE. Oh, all kinds of things.

REUBEN. Like what?

FLOY KATE. Well –

REUBEN. Does she tell you anything about her family or where she's from?

FLOY KATE. No, sir, not much.

REUBEN. Well, what all do you talk about?

(A beat. **FLOY KATE** *turns to face him.)*

FLOY KATE. Daddy, I heard you and Oleta talking. I know where you're heading.

REUBEN. What do you mean where I'm heading?

FLOY KATE. You and Oleta, I heard you last night. I know you think she's the one wanted in the magazine. The one there's a reward out for. But that's not her. She may seem strange to you, but she's not crazy. And she's no escaped criminal.

REUBEN. What makes you so sure?

FLOY KATE. Daddy, she's given me so much encouragement. And shown me things Mama would have shown me. To further myself. And better myself.

REUBEN. What do you mean better yourself?

FLOY KATE. Daddy, she's shown me there's a different world out there.

REUBEN. That reward could save us!

FLOY KATE. We can't falsely accuse her.

REUBEN. She's going to get accused anyway. Oleta'll tell even if we don't.

FLOY KATE. Don't betray her on a suspicion. It'll cost us. It won't cost Oleta anything.

REUBEN. If I don't turn her in, it'll cost us this land. Hear me, girl, land is like family. You don't abandon it when times are hard.

FLOY KATE. But it'll cost our conscience.

REUBEN. I'm sorry, Little Bit, but I can't afford that kind of conscience right now.

FLOY KATE. You can't afford decency?

REUBEN. Floy Kate, girl, my folks staked this land in The Run, settled in and made a crop. They are both buried here along with your mama and my baby son. When he died, your mama liked to never got over it. For two days she wouldn't leave his grave, making a keening cry, like an animal won't abandon a dead newborn. Silhouetted against the flat prairie sky. Blowing in the wind. It put me in mind of a rag caught on barb wire. I went to her and we laid together on that grave as a comfort to each other I expect. And then you came along. I am this land. How can I let it be taken from me?

(The sound of a car pulling up outside.)

(knock at the door)

FLOY KATE. It's Sheriff Trotter.

REUBEN. Come on in.

*(**FLOY KATE** turns and starts for her room.)*

TROT. Reuben.

REUBEN. Floy Kate, aren't you going to offer Trot some coffee?

(as she gets coffee) Have a seat, Trot. What's the latest? Any word on Pretty Boy Floyd?

TROT. Law officers are out on the alert all over the state. They think he may have gone south.

FLOY KATE. Gone South?

REUBEN. A bunch of lowdown scrubs.

TROT. Ain't that the truth? It's an ill wind that blows no good tidings. Reuben, I hate to tell you. Your auction date has been set. Wish you could figure out some way.

(**REUBEN** *looks at* **FLOY KATE**.)

REUBEN. Well – maybe there is a way – I –

FLOY KATE. *(jumping in)* When's the date, Sheriff? For the auction?

TROT. A week from Saturday.

(**OLETA** *comes out of her room, dressed and ready to go to town.*)

OLETA. Where's Miz Arnette?

FLOY KATE. I don't know.

OLETA. How long's she been gone? When will she be back?

TROT. What are you so interested in Miz Arnette for?

OLETA. I can't sleep on account a her bein armed.

TROT. Come on now, girl! Miz Arnette?!

OLETA. She's got a derringer and a dagger.

TROT. How come you to know that?

OLETA. I got ways. What do you think that is hanging off of her belt? She's never without a knife and there's a warrant out for her. You've got to help me find her and get the reward.

TROT. Reward! What reward?

REUBEN. I figure that reward is mine, Oleta.

OLETA. How do you figure that?

REUBEN. She's on my property.

OLETA. Then you've been harboring a fugitive. I seen about her first.

TROT. Any reward goes to whoever finds her first.

OLETA. Then I'm going to get a move on.

TROT. Now hold on here. Just a damn minute. Hold your horses. No point in tearing off in all four different directions at once. You're making a serious accusation here, Oleta. That can get you in a lot of trouble, girl.

OLETA. Not if she's who I think she is.

TROT. You're going off half-cocked on a suspicion.

OLETA. There's no suspicion to it. It's a fact.

TROT. I'll admit Miz Arnette is different alright, but that don't make her an outlaw. That just means she's turned funny.

OLETA. But she's more than crazy.

TROT. What do you have to say about this, Reuben? Has she evidenced any criminal behavior living with you? Anything missing?

FLOY KATE. Of course not.

TROT. Then what's all this about? Reuben? Oleta?

OLETA. I got proof positive.

TROT. How's that? Let's hear your so-called "proof." Trot it out.

OLETA. It's in the magazine.

TROT. What's in the magazine? What magazine?

FLOY KATE. It doesn't sound anything like her.

OLETA. "True Detective." Listen here.

(She reads the wanted notice in the magazine.)

Wanted. At large. Grand Larson. Be on the lookout for white female, approximate age 55. Excapee en route to the Terrell Asylum for the Insane. Warning. Could be a danger to herself and others. Oklahoma, Kansas, New Mexico, Texas, be on the alert. Family offers large reward.

TROT. *(grabbing the magazine)* Let me see that.

OLETA. Now, don't that give the lie to her just being peculiar and harmless?

TROT. Well, I'll have to admit this is usually not the type of escapee seen on a wanted poster.

OLETA. It won't help your reputation none as a lawman if you let her get away.

TROT. It's a sensitive situation. She's got to be handled very carefully under these circumstances.

FLOY KATE. You'll be making a false arrest.

OLETA. You're giving her too much credit for being "sensitive." She knows her way around.

FLOY KATE. What are you saying?

OLETA. I'm saying you're putting a lot at stake to save a monkey and a crazy woman. This ain't her first rodeo. She's been down this road before.

FLOY KATE. You're mistaken. She don't bear the look or actions of an outlaw. She's a Biblical scholar.

REUBEN. But remember, she's said it herself. "The devil hath the power to assume a pleasing shape."

FLOY KATE. She has nothing.

OLETA. That suitcase could have a false bottom.

FLOY KATE. I know this person in the magazine is not her.

OLETA. And I know it is her. Now Trot, what are you going to do about it as a lawman?

TROT. Well, I guess it wouldn't hurt none to round her up and question her.

OLETA. If we can track her. And if it's who I think it is, I want that reward.

(Monkey shreik is heard from offstage.)

*(**OLETA** stalks offstage into the bedroom. She comes back with the wicker suitcase and goes to the outside door.)*

FLOY KATE. What are you up to?

OLETA. She'll never leave without this monkey. We'll have her trapped. I'm going to turn the thing loose.

*(**FLOY KATE** runs to the door after her.)*

FLOY KATE. Stop! You can't turn him loose! It'll kill him.

*(A struggle insues. **OLETA** pushes her back inside. **OLETA** exits wih the cage.)*

OLETA. Shoo!

*(**OLETA** comes back in with the empty cage.)*

That monkey shot out of there like a scalded cat. I'm going to strike out and find her. Trot, you're coming with me.

TROT. *(at the door)* Damn women!

    *(**OLETA** and **TROT** exit.)*

REUBEN. *(turning to **FLOY KATE**)* Where is she?

FLOY KATE. I don't know.

REUBEN. *(taking her by the shoulders)* You know where she goes, Floy Kate.

FLOY KATE. Daddy, I don't know.

REUBEN. You do know. Has she gone over to the rose rocks?

FLOY KATE. Yes. Yes, I do think that's where she went.

REUBEN. You wait here. If she comes back, hold her here until I get here.

FLOY KATE. But I've got to find Little Lucifer.

REUBEN. To hell with that monkey. You wait here.

    (He goes out.)

    *(**FLOY KATE** watches him leave outside the window. When he's good and gone, she quickly snatches up the monkey cage and runs out.)*

FLOY KATE. *(calling from off)* Little Lucifer! Little Lucifer!

    (curtain)

Scene Two

(The stage is empty for a long beat.)

*(**FLOY KATE** comes back in. She has given up the search for Little Lucifer.)*

*(**FLOY KATE** goes into **MIZ ARNETTE**'s room and brings out her valise. She goes back and brings **MIZ ARNETTE**'s things and starts packing them, making several trips.)*

*(**FLOY KATE** takes a beat, thinks. She runs to her room. She brings out the box of her treasures and takes out the little snap purse, the money she's been saving for college and places it in **MIZ ARNETTE**'s suitcase.)*

*(From outside, **FLOY KATE** hears **MIZ ARNETTE**.)*

FLOY KATE. Miz Arnette! Miz Arnette! Come in quick.

MIZ ARNETTE. *(entering)* What a profitable excursion I've had.

FLOY KATE. Miz Arnette, You must…

MIZ ARNETTE. I found signs of all sorts of treasures, some…

FLOY KATE. Please, Please…

MIZ ARNETTE. Many are buried, so, I will have to go back with a trowel.

FLOY KATE. *(taking **MIZ ARNETT** by the shoulders)* Miz Arnett, You must listen to me.

MIZ ARNETTE. What? Why are you behaving like this? *(seeing the suitcase)* What's going on? What are you doing with my things?

FLOY KATE. I packed for you so you can get out of here quicker.

MIZ ARNETTE. What are you talking about? Are you feverish?

FLOY KATE. Little Lucifer is gone and it's cold outside.

MIZ ARNETTE. The weather is of no consequence.

(She rushes into her room and returns empty-handed.)

How did he escape?

FLOY KATE. He didn't escape. Oleta let him out.

MIZ ARNETTE. That stupid, venomous woman. How could she be so cruel? Taking her hostility towards me out on a defenseless animal?

FLOY KATE. That's not why she let him out. She knew you'd be trapped and never go without him. And Miz Arnette, you must go, leave this place.

MIZ ARNETTE. Are you turning me out?

FLOY KATE. They are turning you in.

MIZ ARNETTE. Turning me in? What a peculiar expression. For what?

FLOY KATE. For the reward!

MIZ ARNETTE. What reward?

FLOY KATE. Look.

*(She shows **MIZ ARNETTE** the magazine article.)*

Miz Arnette, they believe this is you.

MIZ ARNETTE. Wanted, suspected of grand larceny?

*(**MIZ ARNETTE** tosses the magazine aside.)*

FLOY KATE. Please, please tell me this isn't you.

*(**MIZ ARNETTE** turns her back to her, head down.)*

*(**FLOY KATE** picks up the magazine.)*

I have to convince them it isn't you. It can't be. Wanted for grand larceny? Escape from an insane asylum? You must tell me, Miz Arnette, it's not you they are after.

*(**MIZ ARNETTE** sits, her head on her arms, folded on the table. After a long pause...)*

MIZ ARNETTE. They have stalked me like an animal and finally run me to ground.

FLOY KATE. So it is you.

MIZ ARNETTE. The deception is theirs. The truth is mine. *(scoffing)* Grand larceny? It is they who have larceny at heart. Since my father's death in Sri Lanka, they have pursued me.

FLOY KATE. What do they want from you?

MIZ ARNETTE. My inheritance. But my father died without a will. In a strange land. He recognized I was clever and inventive. Traits which revealed themselves when I was just a child. He entrusted me with the jewels and gold coins for safekeeping. I've always managed to find a way to secrete them, even when they tracked me to earth and had me confined.

FLOY KATE. So it's true. You were in Terrell Insane Asylum.

MIZ ARNETTE. I escaped en route.

FLOY KATE. How?

MIZ ARNETTE. I just told you. I'm clever and inventive.

(A shriek is heard. MIZ ARNETTE grabs the cage. They run out.)

What on earth are you doing on top of that windmill? Come down at once, my precious beast.

FLOY KATE. Is he wearing his coat?

MIZ ARNETTE. Yes, thank God! Oh, you've torn your jacket. Floy Kate, put him in his cage. I'll get my things.

(She leaves the cage on the porch. MIZ ARNETTE preceeds FLOY KATE back into the house carrying the jacket and picks up the souvenir box. She glances furtivly around. The implication is that she is going to steal the gold piece. She turns her back to the audience. Unseen she places the jacket into Floy Kate's souvenir box.)

(The sound of a train whistle in the distance.)

FLOY KATE. The train! You have to catch that train!

*(**FLOY KATE** hands **MIZ ARNETTE** her suitcase and **MIZ ARNETTE** goes to the door. **MIZ ARNETT** turns back to **FLOY KATE**. Takes her face in her hands...)*

(They hug.)

*(**MIZ ARNETTE** hurries out the door.)*

(The sound of the train whistle coming closer.)

Run, Miz Arnette, run!

(**FLOY KATE** *comes back in. She stands at the door and watches* **MIZ ARNETTE** *leave. She goes to the kitchen table and starts to cry. She goes to the souvenir box; takes out the gold coin so that the audience knows that* **MIZ ARNETTE** *has not stolen it. She then picks up Little Lucifer's jacket.*)

(*She runs to the door to call after* **MIZ ARNETTE**, *but something falls out of the jacket. It is a note.* **FLOY KATE** *picks it up and reads it.*)

FLOY KATE. *(cont.)* "Little Lucifer speaks nor hears nor sees bad tidings,

Yet there is on him many secrets hiding.

For you he leaves his dazzling cloak.

Keep it for yourself alone

Although others may covet its appeal.

Beware to those who try to steal!

Treat it well and secrets it will reveal."

(*Puzzled, she examines the coat. She feels and hears something. She unsnaps the lining. Jewels and gold coins fall out.*)

Daddy!

(*The lights start to fade.* **FLOY KATE** *steps down left. She is now wearing the gold coin on a chain around her neck. She addresses the audience directly.*)

FLOY KATE (VOICE OVER). All was not lost. Only Miz Arnette. Her gift allowed us to keep our land. And I placed second in the essay contest and became a writer. And in 1940 It began to rain. To this day I catch myself looking for Miz Arnette in places impermanent. A traveling carnival, a train station late at night, places that are peopled by the restless shadows of transients, forever on the move. Will-of-the-wisps. Once, while passing by a field, I thought I caught a glimpse of Miz Arnette in a gypsy camp, but when I went in search, the camp had vanished with only the smoke of smoldering embers of their fire left. So has Miz Arnette taken her secrets to the grave or does she still pursue her discoveries in some ancient landscape, still in flight, searching for new adventures? Forever fleeing, thrilled by the chase, and escaped just one step ahead of the sheriff, a bandit queen, continuing to live life on the edge? Whereabouts? Unknown.

"Lives of great men remind us
We can make our lives sublime,
And, departing, leave behind us
Footprints on the sands of time."

FLOY KATE. Robert Browning.

(curtain)

PROPERTIES LIST

Kerosene Lamp: *kitchen table, onstage*
Rags to wipe face: *on table, UC*
Oil cloth table cloth: *covering kitchen table*
Large bucket: *under table, UC*
Bucket for Miz Arnette to collect artifacts
Dipper: *hanging on wall, UL, above stove*
Pot: *on stove, UL*
Pan: *hanging on wall, UL, above stove*
Skillet: *on stove, UL*
Pan of water & wash rags: *on table, UC*
Bundle of Magazines (Modern Screen, True Confessions, Ace Detective, Reader's Digest, Newspaper) page 7: *Off Right*
Bundle of Magazines (True Confessions, Unsolved Detective Stories, Modern Screen): *Off Left*
Bundle of Magazines (Blue True Detective, Photoplay, Redbook, Liberty, Tulsa Tribune (newspaper) page 32: *Off Right*
Coffee Pot: *On stove, UL*
6 Coffee Cups: *on bottom shelf, above table, UC*
Pot holder: *sitting on edge of stove, next to coffee pot*
2 envelopes with foreclosure notice: *Off Right*
Spoons: *(1) in sugar on kitchen table; (1) on table, UC*
Sugar Bowl: *on bottom shelf, above table, UC*
Big Chief tablet: *under table, UC*
Stub pencil: *under table, UC (on – top of big chief tablet)*
Eraser: *under table, UC (on – top of big chief tablet)*
Valise: *Off Right (2)*
Monkey cage: *Off Right*
Rose rock: *Off Right*
Broom: *on – stage, UL, between storeroom and bedroom (propped against wall)*
Dagger: *Off Left (in our case, pre-set in women's dressing room)*
Newspaper clipping advertising room for rent: *in purse, Off Right*
Miz Arnette's papers to scatter on table: *Off Left*
Bible: *Off Left*
Cornbread: *in tins, in stove*
Wet stone: *on bottom shelf, above table, UC*
Socks to darn: *Off Left*
Lucifer's coat with jewels inside: *Off Left*
Floy Kate's treasure box (Picture of Floy Kate and cousins, Jacks, pearl necklace, snap purse, gold piece, Shirley Temple paper doll): *Off Left*
Miz Arnette's ring: *dressing room*
Dictionary – page 40: *Off Left*
Flour and bowl to make paste for comics to paste to wall – page 40: *flour: on table, UC; bowl: under table, UC*
Comic pages to paste to wall – page 40: *on floor, by stove, UL*

One rag for window sill: *in windowsill (1)*
Things to put in Miz Arnette's suitcase: *in suitcases, Off Right*
Note in Lucifer's jacket: *Off Left*
Cigarette holder for Miz Arnette & Turkish Cigarettes – page 27: *Off Left*
Cigarette ash tray: *Off Left*
Muff and gun: *Off Left*
Knife for whittling: *Men's dressing room*
Handkerchief: *Off Right*

COSTUME PLOT

FLOY KATE
Act I-1
  Shirt
  Blue coveralls
  Extra long brown belt
  Socks
  Brown oxfords
  Cowboy hat
  Jacket
  Red kerchief
Act I-2
  Same as above
Act I-3
  Same as above
Act II-!
  Flower sack cotton dress
  Sweater
  Bobby socks
  Same brown oxfords
  Same brown belt
Act II-2
  Same as Act II-1

RUEBEN
Act I-1
  Plaid shirt
  Faded red long john shirt
  Work pants
  Suspenders
  Socks
  Brown boots
  Cowboy hat
  Cattleman's Jacket
  Blue kerchief
Act I-2
  Change plaid shirt
  Change long john undershirt
  All else same as above
Act I-3
  Same as above
Act II-1
  Different shirt
  Leather vest
  Different pants with suspenders

    Same boots
    Same hat
    Same coat
Act II-2
    Same as Act II-1

OLETA

Act I-1
    Dress
    Heels
    Sweater
    Seamed cotton hose
    Coat
    Hat
    purse

Act I-2
    Another Dress
    Another sweater
    Same Shoes

Act I-3
    Same dress as above
    Same sweater
    Same shoes
    Same coat as Act I-1

Act II-!
    Chennile robe
    Slip
    Same shoes as Act I-1
    Change to same as Act I-1

Act II-2
    Same as Act II-1

MIZ ARNETTE

Costumes should reflect her world travels

Act I-1
    Cape
    Black Dress
    Brown overskirt from India
    Brown Jacket from India
    Black oxfords with a heel
    Jewelry (Gold chain with a medallion around her neck, Gold slave bracelets on each wrist, Rings on each finger (one agate with a fly embedded in it)
    A man's brown belt with a dagger hanging from it
    Beige cotton stockings
    A purse to hang across her chest
    Handkerchief

Act I-2
    Same black dress
    Chinese overlay
    Same jewelry as above
    Same shoes and stockings
Act I-3
    Lush but worn robe over black dress
    Chinese slippers
    Same jewelry as above
Act II-!
    Same black dress
    Short kimono top
    Flowered velvet skirt
    Same jewelry as above
    Same brown belt with dagger
    Same oxfords with beige cotton stockings
Act II-2
    Same as Act II-1

SHERIFF TROTTER
Act I-1 and throughout
    Khaki shirt
    Khaki pants
    Cowboy hat
    Cowboy boots
    Belt
    Holster and gun
    Long coat
    Men's white handkerchief
    Sheriff badge